COUNTDOWN
to the
SHEFFIELD BLITZ

By the Sheffield Blitz Group

Compiled by Neil Anderson

Sheffield Corporation Waterworks staff were
sent to London to help with Blitz damage.

The Countdown to War in Sheffield

1932 Sheffield City Hall opens in Barker's Pool. This building was originally conceived as a legacy to the local men that died in the Great War. It was meant to be part of the healing process – a way to bring the city together. Little did they know that it would soon be caught up in the countdown to an even bigger worldwide conflict, and would itself be in the front line of battle.

1933 Nazis come to power in Germany.

1934 15,000 protest in Barker's Pool against British Union of Fascists meeting at Sheffield City Hall.

1935 Sheffield's steel mills working at full capacity to re-arm the country.

1938 Future Prime Minister Winston Churchill speaks at Sheffield City Hall.

Gas attack drills occur in Sheffield; scores of buildings are requisitioned for war use and public air raid shelters; children are being prepared for evacuation.

1939 February – First Anderson Shelters arrive in the region.

August 29 – Ecclesall Junior School reopens after the summer break "under the shadow of imminent war".

August 31 – The Star announces 'Evacuation of schools will begin tomorrow.'Ecclesall Junior School, in accordance with instructions received by telegram, closes tonight until further notice, to assist with evacuation of children from Neepsend C.E. School.

September 1 – Clifford Church of England School, Psalter Lane, is closed all day to enable teachers to help with evacuation of children of Cathedral School.

Taking a call on behalf of the
National Fire Service.

Contents

Foreword

Neil Anderson

Neil Anderson's grandmother, Dorothy Glover (right). Author of the memoir that started the Sheffield Blitz legacy campaign.

I often wonder what my grandmother would think of her inadvertent legacy.

She wasn't one to dwell on the past, so it came as quite a surprise, following her death in 2009, to unearth a lengthy memoir tucked away in a drawer. The one thing it did dwell on was life in the city in World War Two and the Sheffield Blitz in 1940; it was those memories that set off an amazing chain of events that culminated in the unveiling of an exhibition, the launch of this book and a forthcoming walk around key WW2 sites within the city centre.

The Sheffield Blitz didn't appear to have bothered my grandmother too much; it was the hours on end spent with the neighbours in the communal air raid shelter on Coningsby Road in Fir Vale that really seemed to wind her up. That, and the interruption of nights out at her nearby, beloved Sunbeam Cinema – where air raid warnings were regularly causing her to miss the second half of all her favourite films (not to mention the money it was costing her).

Like everyone else in Sheffield, she became quite blasé about the sirens, as the actual attacks never seemed to come, until December 12th, 1940, that is.

It wasn't until I started researching the bombings that I began to understand the extent of the death and destruction: nearly a tenth of the city's population made homeless, over two thousand killed or wounded, hardly a suburb left unscathed.

Everything I'd ever read about the attacks pointed to Hitler wanting to wipe out the city's East End – hub of armaments production. But if that was the case, why on earth were suburbs like Dore, Totley, Millhouses and Gleadless being attacked?

When I was researching my 'Sheffield's Date With Hitler' book, I found some German bombing maps of Sheffield. Though the factories were marked down as targets, they were marked as secondary targets. Primary targets appeared to be hospitals, schools, railways and more – which led me to suggest the Sheffield Blitz was far more of a terror raid designed to bomb the population into submission.

Two nights of blanket bombing later and the opposite happened: Sheffielders became more defiant than ever. Their stoical nature was even held up as an example to the whole country by Prime Minister Winston Churchill.

Interest in my book truly took me by surprise – with the BBC even turning it into a documentary: 'Sheffield – The Forgotten Blitz.' By that time I'd already decided there should be more to remember the attacks. The BBC's title truly brought home the lack of recognition.

I'm indebted to Richard Godley and Bill Bevan, who helped secure £81,000 of Heritage Lottery Funding in 2015 and have worked with me throughout the Sheffield Blitz 75th project.

I was truly humbled to help unveil the first permanent exhibition to the Sheffield Blitz, which now sits inside the city's National Emergency Services Museum at West Bar. It contains scores of rare and original Blitz-related objects and photos, Second World War emergency vehicles, oral history

Total devastation on High Street after the first night to of the Sheffield Blitz.

7

Top: Waingate devastation. **Above:** ARP Ambulance Service workers in action.

recordings from survivors, and film footage, as well as the fire brigade's original map of bomb sites across the city. The centrepiece is the last surviving fire engine that was on duty on both nights of the Sheffield Blitz.

This book would not have been possible if it hadn't been for the fantastic group of volunteers that have worked tirelessly on research and undertaking scores of interviews with survivors. Their work has helped provide a month-by-month, day-by-day, hour-by-hour countdown to the Sheffield Blitz – something that has never been done before.

More information on Sheffield Blitz 75th from: https://sheffieldblitz.wordpress.com or follow @SheffieldBlitz75th

More information on the National Emergency Services Museum from: www.emergencymuseum.org.uk

'Sheffield's Date With Hitler' is available from: www.acmretro.com

A legacy to the great Doug Lightning

It is with great sadness that I acknowledge Douglas Lightning – the last surviving firefighter from the Sheffield Blitz – didn't get to see the culmination of our project.

He was an inspiration to all that met him and he generously gave his time and support to the cause.

You can hear him describe his awe-inspiring experiences, fighting the fires of the Sheffield Blitz, at the exhibition with Sheffield's National Emergency Services Museum.

CHAPTER 1

Britain is at War
September 3rd, 1939

Britain declared war on Germany on September 3rd, 1939. The sombre, though hardly unexpected, news was delivered that morning by Prime Minister Neville Chamberlain

German troops had crossed the Polish border two days earlier and unleashed the world's first 'blitzkrieg.'

Poland's troops were totally unprepared for this new kind of warfare.

Both Britain and France were obliged to help Poland. Sadly the situation was already beyond redemption.

Warsaw surrendered on September 27th, following the Soviets marching into Poland from the East. At that point the Russians were German allies.

The British government had delivered an ultimatum to

The junction of Surrey St, Pinstone St and Fargate in the mid-1930s.

Germany – start withdrawing troops by 11am on September 3rd or face war.

They didn't withdraw; in fact they didn't bother responding to the message at all.

It's hard to imagine what it must have been like hearing the news that September morning.

Families across Sheffield huddled around their wirelesses to hear the news as it was broadcast at 11am.

"I am speaking to you from the Cabinet Room at 10 Downing Street," said Chamberlain.

"This morning the British Ambassador in Berlin handed the German government a final note stating that, unless we heard from them by 11 o'clock that they were prepared at once to withdraw their troops from Poland, a state of war would exist between us. I have to tell you now that no such undertaking has been received, and that consequently this country is at war with Germany.

"You can imagine what a bitter blow it is to me that all my long struggle to win peace has failed. Yet I cannot believe that there is anything more or anything different that I could have done and that would have been more successful.

"Up to the very last it would have been quite possible to have arranged a peaceful and honourable settlement between Germany and Poland, but

Adolf Hitler and high ranking Nazis – their attention would turn to Sheffield in December 1940.

Hitler would not have it. He had evidently made up his mind to attack Poland, whatever happened, and although he now says he put forward reasonable proposals which were rejected by the Poles, that is not a true statement.

"The proposals were never shown to the Poles, nor to us, and though they were announced in a German broadcast on Thursday night, Hitler did not wait to hear.

"His action shows convincingly that there is no chance of expecting that this man will ever give up his practice of using force to gain his will. He can only be stopped by force.

"We and France are today, in fulfilment of our obligations, going to the aid of Poland, who is so bravely resisting this wicked and unprovoked attack upon her people. We have a clear conscience- we have done all that any country could do to establish peace.

"The situation in which no word given by Germany's ruler could be trusted, and no people or country could feel itself safe, has become intolerable. And now that we have resolved to finish it I know that you will play your part with calmness and courage.

"At such a moment as this the assurances of support which we have received from the empire are a source of profound encouragement to us.

"When I have finished speaking, certain detailed announcements will be made on behalf of the government. Give these your closest attention. The government have made plans under which it will be possible to carry on work of the nation in the days of stress and strain that may be ahead...

"Now may God bless you all. May he defend the right. For it is evil things that we shall be fighting against- brute force, bad faith, injustice, oppression and persecution- and against them I am certain that right will prevail."

Mrs K. Toulson:

"We were evacuated to Skegness, a bed and breakfast on Roman Bank, my mother, myself and baby brother. We didn't stay long as my mother wanted to go home to dad."

Joyce Green:

"We were all traumatized by the rise of Nazism. You knew war was going to happen – it was just a question of time. "I was already questioning Chamberlain's earlier appeasement policy – he'd played right into Hitler's hands and now we were all going to pay."

Opposite, top: Prime Minister Neville Chamberlin returns from Germany with his infamous 'Peace In Our Time' paper.

Opposite, bottom: Sir Oswald Moseley (second from left) with his chief organisers at Sheffield City Hall's British Union Fascist meeting that brought out 15,000 protestors in 1934.

Below: The city's home guard in training in 1941.

Joe Ellis:

"My mum burst into tears and hugged my sister and me as we stood in front of the radio. My dad tried to reassure her that everything would be okay but she wasn't convinced – and neither was he. I can still see the look in her eyes as she tried to hide her fear from us. I'll never ever forget that day. How we hated Hitler."

Dorothy Welsby:

"My father survived the Somme in World War One. He was one of the few survivors from the doomed Sheffield City Battalion. Though he knew war was coming, he was still devastated to know it had come so quickly after the Great War. I can still remember the feeling of absolute dread that descended on our house in Fir Vale."

Lillian Clay:

"World War Two broke out when I was eighteen. I can always remember when they announced it on the radio. I was at my mum's in Hillsborough.

She said: 'God help us all.'
"I remember we had to carry our gasmasks about everywhere. I had a gas-cot for my baby."

Gas attack drill

CHAPTER 2

Sheffield's first
Air Raid Warning
September 4th, 1939

It was 3.30am on the morning of September 4th, 1939, that the first air raid siren of the war was heard over Sheffield, literally hours after war was declared. It rang out for half an hour. Thankfully it was a false alarm – there were no bombs dropped.

The south coast came nearer to attack a couple of days later. A German raid was reported as heading their way on September 6th, 1939.

On this occasion, no bombs were dropped again. It is thought the bombers were even driven back, or unfavourable weather caused them to do a u-turn.

Like in Sheffield, it gave an early taste of the eerie sound of an air raid siren; a sound that would become an almost daily occurrence for the next few years.

The first Anderson Shelter was built in 1938. It was commissioned by the British Home Office in preparation for WW2 and designed by William Paterson and Oscar Carl Kerrison.

The shelters started being distributed to homes in Sheffield in February 1939 – a full six months before war broke out.

By the outbreak of war, 1.5million had already been distributed. Another 2.1 million were constructed in gardens across the country during the course of the war. Each one could hold up to six people and they were incredibly strong. The figures speak for themselves- around 500,000 people were killed in German cities as a result of allied bombing. Germans bombs killed 90% less in the UK, around 50,000.

The city had numerous false alarms and small raids in the run up to the attacks.

The population, unsurprisingly, got quite blasé about hearing the sirens.

Opposite: Sheffield children being evacuated at Victoria Station – the city ended up with one of the lowest evacuation rates anywhere in the country.

In the beginning they'd rush out of their cinema seats and head for the nearest public shelter. As the months dragged on, and the predicted major raids didn't arrive, they started to ignore the sirens altogether.

Newspaper censorship stopped a lot of information being published about the German raids, so it's often down to personal diaries to provide a picture of what the city went through night after night.

Mildred Smith lived at the top house in Forres Road, Crookes. She lived through the war living with her parents. Her house had a view right across the city. She worked at Thomas Ward's and was his personal secretary. She kept a diary her entire life.

Below is the first of several extracts reproduced throughout this book.

1939, 6th Sept   Clifford Church of England School, Psalter Lane introduces home teaching.

1940, 8th Jan	Clifford Church of England School, Psalter Lane - School reopened this morning. Nineteen admissions. No. on the roll 101. Miss Jolly inspected air raid shelters in the afternoon. Air raid shelter practice taken Tuesday, Wednesday, Thursday of the week commencing 8th Jan 1940. Gas mask drill on Thursday.

John Unsworth remembers preparing for the worst

"I was born in 1930 and, throughout World War II, I lived in a rented terrace house at 162 Blair Athol Road, Banner Gross, Ecclesall, Sheffield.

These houses were built when cars were a rarity, so there was no garage space. This was a time when owning your own house was also unusual, at least for working class people. The houses were all attached and ran from Glenalmond Road to Huntingtower Road. Each group of four houses had a 'passage' running up the middle that divided into two 'yards.' Our 'front door' was actually in the middle of the passage, which had a bathroom for each of the middle houses over it (but originally, no indoor toilet).

The government decided that, as we were very vulnerable - as a city making vital munitions - we should be given the opportunity to have a means of shelter from bombs, and were given a choice of protection.

We were told that we could have a corrugated iron 'Anderson' air raid shelter in the tiny back garden, a 'Morrison' shelter (a reinforced metal table) inside, or an escape route from our cellar. We chose the last and men arrived to knock holes through the cellar walls into 164 and 160 and thereon down the road. The idea was that, should we be bombed, it would be possible to move through these square openings, each about 2 feet square, from one end of the road to the other. They had doors and bolts on them, but during an air raid, they were all opened. Mrs. Stanney at No. 164, made a poor decision because she was never able to use the outside 'Anderson' shelter that had been sunk into her garden, as it became water logged because of a stream running underground down the hill. She would, however, have been able to benefit from the 'escape route' had it been necessary."

Soldiers taking time out in Sheffield.

20th June   As a result of last night's air raid warning the attendance this morning at Ecclesall Junior School is poor - only 64%

28th August   Ecclesall Junior School - owing to air raid during last night, there was no morning school. The new regulation became operative and we opened school from 1pm to 5pm.

The Sheffield Gun Defended Area (GDA)

Sheffield was no stranger to anti-aircraft defences. During the First World War Sheffield became the first city outside London to receive anti-aircraft guns and searchlights operated by the Royal Naval Volunteer Reserve. Although the guns had failed to defend the city against a Zeppelin raid on the night of 25 September 1916; low cloud made it impossible for the gun crews to visually identify and engage the airship; the city would see the return of anti-aircraft guns and searchlights once again in the Second World War.

As a major city and important industrial centre, Sheffield was provided with an extensive network of anti-aircraft defences. These defences consisted of anti-aircraft batteries; each with four 4.5in or 3.7in guns; searchlight batteries and barrage balloons. These defences made up the Sheffield Gun Defended Area (GDA) which stretched from Doncaster, across Rotherham to Sheffield, with further defences sited as far South as Clay Cross.

Anti-aircraft guns were the main active defence of the GDA; while Royal Observer Corps posts, barrage balloons and searchlights were considered passive defences. Active and passive defences worked together to defend potential targets of the Luftwaffe.

Sheffield's defences were co-ordinated from a central command centre. Reports from Royal Observer Corps posts would be telephoned back to the command centre, indicating the height, direction and number of aircraft in a raid. This information would then be used to co-ordinate the defence of the city and raise the alarm of the incoming raid. The defences would then go into action.

Generally, anti-aircraft batteries were concentrated around important or vulnerable infrastructure, usually industrial centres and factories, as well as likely approaches of enemy aircraft. A battery consisted of four gun emplacements, each housing a single 3.7in or 4.5in anti-aircraft gun. A command bunker was often sited centrally close to the gun emplacements. The battery's fire was co-ordinated from the command bunker using a height finder and a predictor; the predictor calculated the correct elevation and direction for the guns based on the user's inputs. The firing solution was then sent via cable to the gun emplacements, where dials on the guns allowed the gunners to correctly sight their weapon and fire. The command bunker was also responsible for plotting information provided from central command, allowing them to track raids in the vicinity for interception. Frequent reports from the battery would be sent back to the command centre via telephone to help build up an accurate picture of the incoming air raids.

Batteries would often be sited to provide interlocking arcs of fire, essentially allowing more than one battery to fire at the same area of sky simultaneously, concentrating fire on an enemy formation.

Barrage balloons were also deployed in and around potential targets. These large hydrogen filled balloons were sent aloft, often flying at around 5,000 to 6,000 feet in the air. The balloon itself wasn't particularly dangerous to aircraft. However, the cable it trailed was. The cable would snag the wings of an aircraft, eventually ripping the wing from the aircraft. The main purpose of the barrage balloon was to force enemy aircraft to a higher altitude, making their bombing less accurate. The fire of nearby anti-aircraft batteries was usually pre-registered in concentrated barrages above the barrage balloons, creating a pre-prepared killing zone in the sky.

On 20 November 1940, Sheffield had recorded sixteen 4.5in, eight 3.7in static and four 3.7in mobile anti-aircraft guns defending its skies. Following the raids on the city on 12 and 15 December, records show an additional sixteen mobile 3.7in guns were brought in to bolster the existing anti-aircraft guns by 18 December 1940 (Statistics from *Dobinson's AA Command*).

Today, little survives of Sheffield's wartime anti-aircraft defences. The foundation of a single gun emplacement in Parkwood Springs is the only structure to remain.

Sources:

Dobinson, C., 2001. AA Command. Methuen Publishing Ltd.

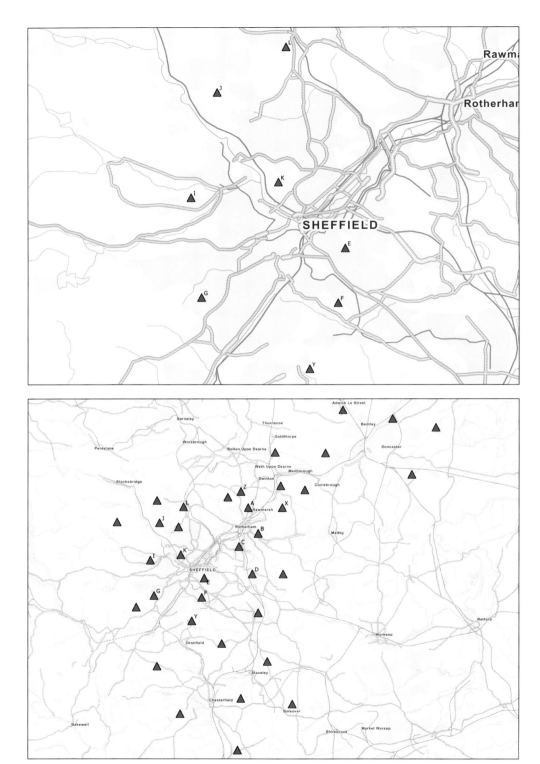

Top: Sheffield WW2 Batteries (1940). **Bottom:** Sheffield GDA.

CHAPTER 3

London Blitz Starts
September 7th, 1940

The London Blitz on Britain began in earnest nearly a year to the day into the war. The Germans attacked the capital on September 7th. The raid left 430 dead and 1,600 injured.

The capital city was bombed for 57 consecutive nights, with many daytime raids.

Birmingham

The city holds the unenviable title of the third most bombed city, after London and Liverpool. The first major raid took place in August 1940; with more following in September, October and November of that year.

One of Birmingham's most important factories, the Birmingham Small Arms (BSA) works, was hit and 53 workers killed.

Bristol

The coastal city had already received numerous smaller air raids, but November 24th, 1940 will always be the date that truly changed the face of Bristol.

German bombers dropped 1,540 tons of high explosives and 12,500 incendiaries. The raid killed 207 people and left a further 187 injured.

Many of Bristol's historic buildings were destroyed, with scores of unexploded bombs left behind.

Coventry

German bombers dropped 503 tons of high explosives and 30,000 incendiary bombs on the city in a devastating raid on November 14th/15th, 1940. The medieval cathedral was destroyed. 568 people were killed with a further 850 seriously injured Almost a third of the city's housing stock was made uninhabitable, with 35% of its shops destroyed. With a relatively small population of 200,000, it was said that everyone knew someone that had been killed or injured.

A new verb coventrieren – 'to Coventrate' – was adopted by the Germans to describe the level of destruction.

Southampton

The city was hit hard on the nights of November 23rd and November 30th. The second raid lasted six hours with 800 tons of high explosives being dropped. The Auxiliary Fire Service (AFS) were short of men, and reinforcements had to be brought in quickly from nearby areas.

The authorities struggled to cope in the aftermath with water, gas and electricity cut off across great swathes of the city.

Liverpool

The city and much of the Merseyside area was the most bombed area in Britain outside of the capital.

November 28th/29th saw it hit by 350 tons of high explosive bombs. The run-up to Christmas – December 20th-23rd – saw four nights of consecutive bombing.

The heavy raids continued into 1941 (early May saw eight days of heavy bombing).

The docks were the main target, but the streets of terraced houses that surrounded the area and housed the dockers and their families were also devastated.

Manchester

The city endured the heaviest raids on December 22nd/23rd and December 23rd/24th, 1940. The bombing destroyed the Free Trade Hall, Smithfield Market and St Anne's Church. More than 8,000 homes were destroyed or left uninhabitable.

Many of Manchester's firemen and civil defence workers were still attending to stricken Liverpool after rushing to help following the devastating raid on their neighbouring city.

Cardiff

Bombed on January 2nd, 1941, it marked the start of a series of raids on docks that were vital in maintaining British supply lines.

Bombers returned again early March.

Portsmouth

The naval base was hit almost every four weeks during early 1941. Its heaviest raid was on January 10th/11th when the Germans dropped 140 tons of high explosives and 40,000 incendiaries.

Hull

The north east of England was another target in early 1941. The coastal port

Civilians were being trained to be ready for gas attacks in the months leading up to the outbreak of war – thankfully the real thing never came.

suffered two heavy raids in March and then was badly hit again on May 8th/9th. Hull was bombed again in June, after the worst of the Blitz attacks were thought to be over.

Plymouth

Its docks and naval base made it a major target and in March/April 1941 it was hit by a number of major raids. More than 900 people were killed and 40,000 made homeless. The city lost its historic Guildhall and, like Sheffield, main shopping streets were badly hit.

Clydebank

The industrial area west of Glasgow was subject to one of the most intense bombing raids across two nights. March 13th/14th saw 35,000 of Clydebank's 50,000 become homeless. The Clydebank Blitz was cited as "a major disaster" by the Scottish Regional Commissioner.

Belfast

The city's docks and shipyards were the primary targets but, as in similar raids, residential areas were also badly hit.

Belfast experienced its first big raid on April 7th/8th. The bombers returned a few days later – on April 15th.

CHAPTER 4

Final countdown to Sheffield Blitz - Mildred's Diary

Sheffield Corporation staff repair damage.

1940

Saturday, 18th August

The bombs came tonight for the first time while we were all asleep

Monday, 19th

Bombs again, and the rattle of guns.

Tuesday 20th

Peace for us at least. They came near, but heard nothing. It was a stormy night, and windy.

Friday, 23rd

We all got up this morning congratulating ourselves on a peaceful night and found we had all slept thro' another bombing fracas. They came early in the morning!

Saturday, 24th

10.30pm sirens went off. Went to bed at 12am but up again. Bombs dropped at 1.30am.

Sunday, 25th

Tired of getting up. Bombs again at 4am. Slept thro' the rattle of guns all night. Up late, tired and drowsy.
A plane came round about 2am again, Jerry I think. We all stayed in bed.

Monday, 26th

At bedtime, we laughed and said we would go and have 10 minutes sleep

Tuesday, 27th

Alone in the house, siren went at 11pm, all clear at 3.30am. All windows were smashed in in one district and a board chalked up saying "No window cleaners wanted here!"

Wednesday, 28th

Sirens at 10pm. All clear at 11.30pm. To bed and at 1.30am crashing bombs lit my room. All went downstairs in the dark passage. Planes buzzing over nearly an hour. Heard screech of bombs passing over us. Long suspense was terrible. Clear at 3.30am. What a night. Worst one up to now.

Thursday, 29th August	Saw broken windows in town and havoc all on Sheaf Street. Smashed windows are far as High Street/trying to get to the railways. One bomb had fallen at Sandygate and Crookesmoor.
Friday, 30th	Jerry buzzing round at 10.15pm. Sirens screamed just when he was overheard. A few bombs, all clear about 2am when there was another warning. Bombs again. We went to bed at 4am too indifferent and tired.
Saturday, 31st	Planes about 10.30pm again – Jerry mucking about till about 3-ish again.
Sunday, 1st Sept	Went to see brother at Horse Guards Parade. Saw the damage (doesn't say what damage). Slept all afternoon. Jerry round 11pm, bomb at 2am, to be around 3.30am. What a week! *(Just a little comment at the bottom of the week's diary:* "I now get undressed in a morning to wash. My bed is a chair and I read in bed – ha,ha! I have not been undressed for 3 nights; a saving in nighties. I wash at night for the morning before!"*)*
Monday, 2nd	Jerry here tonight at 9.45pm. Sirens and all clear about 12.30am.
Tuesday, 3rd	To bed at 8.30pm. Woken up by 3 bombs at 12am. Back to bed, up at 3am and back. Edgar forgotten his teeth (Edgar was her brother)
Wednesday, 4th	To bed at 10.30 pm. Bombs at 11.45pm, till 2am. Back again to bed. Thud at 5am, after all clear bells.
Thursday, 5th	Sirens at 10.30pm, to bed – up – to bed – up – oh la! - how many times? All clear and round comes Jerry. Jerry also round at breakfast, 9am.
Friday, 6th	Sirens at 9pm, clear at 9.30pm.

Saturday, 7th	Sirens at 11pm, clear at 11.30pm. Fairly good night.
Sunday, 8th	Went to Wyming Brook with friends. Then to Molly's cottage at night. Sirens at 10.30pm, but a good night's sleep. There was the first rumour this morning of an invasion. Molly's father and brother had been called out at 1am, Sunday morning. Soldiers coming packed up to Wyming Brook, then cyclists who were turned back. Buses too.
Monday, 9th	Sirens at 5am. Decent Night.
Tuesday, 10th	Ditto. 12.30am to 1am. Dreamt I was a nun with 3 others going to a monastery singing 'Silent night' alone. Other two's caroling changed to realistic siren warning. Woke with the song still in my ears.
Wednesday, 11th	Went 4 times between 12.30am and 2am. What a night.
Thursday, 12th	Sirens once.

Bomb damage on the Godfrey Dam embankment, 14th March, 1941.

Saturday, 14th September	Three of us to Bamford, Bradwell, Great Hucklow and back to Castleton. Tea at Hollowford. Invasion rumours again. Sirens at 8.30pm as I came home.
Sunday, 15th	Good night last night. Rex and friend came with funny stories about 10 bombs dropping. Turned out to be their dog jumping overhead down 10 stairs!!
Monday, 16th	Sirens 8.15pm tonight, earlier every night. This is supposed to be Invasion Day – "Der Tag"
Wednesday, 18th	Sirens 9.30pm to 10.30pm.
Thursday, 19th	No sirens, but heard plane for a short time.
Friday, 20th	Plane nearly on house top.
Saturday, 21st	Went to Cordwell Valley and saw bomb wreckage. Sirens 11.30pm to 12am and bombs
Sunday, 22nd	Sirens 2am – 2.30am. No sound.
Monday, 23rd	Sirens 11.30pm to 12am. We didn't get up!
Thursday, 26th	No sign of anything, then bombs dropping at 9.15pm. Warning came after the bombs!

Things died down after this. A home watch duty was done mid October, Edgar continued to do Home Guard exercises, lights were turned out on buses at night, but life carried on as normal, until:

Monday, 14th October	Incendiaries were dropped all round Ecclesfield and Wincobank.
Tuesday, 22nd	Bombs last night at 8.30pm.
Saturday, 26th	Went into office, on to Slaters for bang-up tea – what a tea! Howls of laughter – then bombs. We never heard seven of them. Home for 11pm after all clear. Bombs at 7.30am.

Sunday, 27th	Heard plane tonight.
Monday, 28th	Plane over at 7am this morning. They got him!
Wednesday, 13th November	Went alone to Hippodrome, enjoying film with sirens went at 6.15pm. Walked all the way home and all clear.
Tuesday, 19th	All round the fire at home and suddenly shelling at 9.35pm. Pa lost his bacca! No bombs dropped, no sirens, but tiles loose (afterwards we found they were not ours!
Wednesday, 20th	9.30pm plane and sirens. Clear at midnight. Guns heard outside Sheffield at 4am.
Friday, 22nd	Sirens 3 times, plane at 8.15pm, sirens at 8.45pm to 9.30pm. Then 11.45pm to 12.50am the third time, and 3am to nearly 4am. What a night!

Bomb damage on the Godfrey Dam embankment, 14th March, 1941.

Rare photos of Sheffield City Council's Waterworks and subsequent wartime bomb damage. The main picture shows Sheffield men helping in London to replace bomb damaged infrastructure.

25.10.40.

4092.

| **Thursday, 28th November** | Sirens 7.10pm to 4am. Planes across all night, bags of them. No bombs. |
| **Wednesday, 11th December** | Sirens 11.30pm to 12.30am. Again 3am to 5.45am. Nothing dropped. |

Sheffield Corporation staff repair damage.

CHAPTER 5

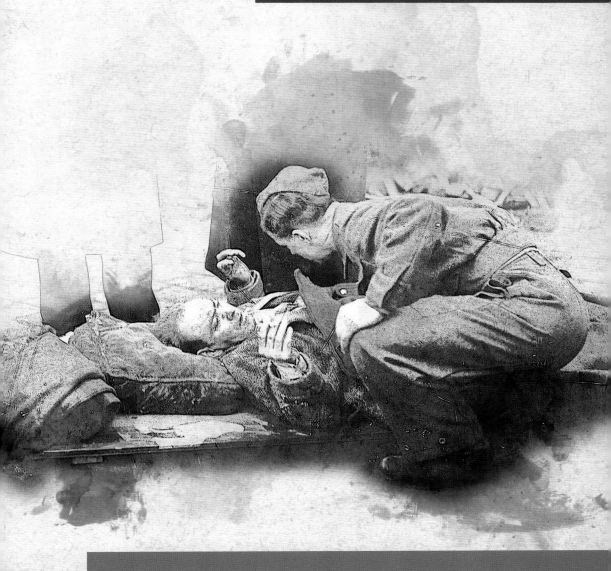

Sheffield Blitz - Day One
December 12th, 1940

Time finally ran out for the city of Sheffield on Thursday, December 12th, 1940. By the early evening, thousands of people were heading back into the city centre. The cinemas were busy, the dancehalls were busy and city's pubs and hotels were packed to capacity.

When the sirens rang out at 7pm, people didn't bat an eyelid. When the sound of the city's Ack Ack guns cranked into life, people quickly realised this might be a raid like no other.

Thursday, 12th Dec	EVE OF BLACK FRIDAY! 7pm sirens, and bombs and gunfire straight after. No space. 11pm to 1am terrific. Right on to 4.15am. Nine hours of solid gunfire and bombs. House creaked and rattled, bits dropped and rolled.

Douglas Kay:

"My older brother and I went to the Heeley Picture Palace to see a Mickey Rooney film, and about halfway through a notice appeared on the screen telling us the sirens had just sounded and anybody wanting to leave should do so. Mickey was just climbing over the coal bunker on the train to get at the baddies. We looked round and some girls just sat there so we had to stay too.

'When the picture had finished we went out into the foyer and a woman and some kids were all crying. We ignored them, opened the glass swing door and heard this whistling screaming sound. We both took off like 100 yard sprinters and dived under a lorry.

'We lay there for a while when I was suddenly lifted onto a man's shoulder like a sack of coal and dumped down on a wooden bench under the railway arches. I sat there, numb, when I realised Geoff was still out there. I pulled the Policeman's cuff, he turned round, face as black as coal and looked at me with bleary eyes. "What is it

lad?" "My brother is under that lorry outside." "Is he? I'll go and get him," and so he did. He had just recovered from hitting his head on the lorry's steel frame.

"We sat there, no drinks or anything, and wondered about our house and mother. Eventually the all-clear sounded and everybody shuffled out into a cloudless full moon night and we walked up Chesterfield Road passing a large crater in Little London area where people sat at the edge trying to get water from the burst pipe. We got as far as Derbyshire Lane when mother appeared a look of enormous relief on her face.

"My grandmother was in the shelter with us the night after and sat on the bed telling us about the beautiful sky she could see from her bed. She lived alone in a large house on Broadfield Road and, by sheer luck she got up to go to the toilet when an incendiary bomb came through the roof, through the attic, straight through the bed she had been lying on, and into the cellar where it fizzled out. My father and Geoff went to have a look and repair the hole if there was one - grandmother was old and could have just invented the story - but it turned out to be perfectly true. She died a few months later.

"Geoff and I went into town the next morning, after the Thursday raid. We lived in Meersbrook, so walked down Chesterfield Road, London Road and up the Moor. About halfway up the Moor, we saw a policeman shuffling round a bombed-out Bank site, Yorkshire Penny, I think. Curious, I also kicked a brick to one side and there I saw a small cloth bag, Geoff nudged me and nodded his head towards the policeman, and then sat down on a bent steel girder looking all innocent with his foot on the prize. The policeman wandered off, and Geoff picked up the bag, peered inside and pulled out a handful of sixpenny bits. We were rich, we could buy some food.

"We walked to the top of the Moor and there, lying in the middle of the road, was a fireman. We dashed over, along with a middle-aged woman, and tried to lift him but he was too heavy. By sheer luck one of the burnt-out shops had been a bedding shop, where we found a couple of scorched blankets which we eased under his body and used to drag him onto the pavement. There was a stall nearby run by a women's organisation, giving away tea and sandwiches, so we got in the queue and took some over to the fireman who seemed to have recovered a bit, so he managed to drink the tea and eat a scone and thanked us. We got back in the queue but the woman told us we could only have one serving and she had seen us before."

Cheryl Clarke:

"I was born the year of peace 1945. My sister was born 1939 just as the war had started. My mother used to tell us the story of the Blitz. On the night of the Blitz, she was living in Woodhouse. My grandmother - her mother - had a sweet shop on Penistone Road, opposite Hillsborough Park. My mother set off on the morning after the Blitz, with my sister in her pram to walk to Hillsborough Park to see if my grandmother was alright. However, she had only managed to get into the town centre, quite near to the Moor, when she was stopped by the military. They told her that the area was a no-go. She said there were trams that were still blazing, and that most of the Moor was flattened and on fire - a terrifying sight. The military was everywhere trying to assist people and tending to the injured, etc. One of the soldiers asked her where she was heading. She told them she was going to Hillsborough to check on my grandmother and asked if the area had been badly bombed. The soldier said it had taken a hit, but wasn't sure of the extent of the damage. She was terrified. However, he bundled her, and the pram with my sister in it, onto the lorry then he took them as near to Hillsborough as was considered safe. Thank God everyone was safe and well, although really frightened."

Angela Maura Armitage-Owen:

"Mum said that her and her parents were in the shelter luckily, as the chimney came through the roof straight through the attic and landed in her parents' bed. Also great-gran's house, three doors down, was totally bombed, big crater in the road and a tram was half in and out. This was all on Abbeydale Road, yards down from the cinema."

Joan Griffin:

"Dad reinforced the cellar and it was really, really good. We had a double bed down there. There was the coal at one side because it was a big cellar and there was a meat safe cos there was no fridges in those days. It was quite cold down that cellar, I don't think we had any heating but we'd an eiderdown, you know.

"I think it was about seven o'clock at night when the sirens went, I'm not quite sure, and we went down the cellar and then it wasn't long before it really started and it was just one continual *screaming of bombs coming down. It seemed to get nearer and nearer to us, until it was practically on top of us, and every bomb that came down you felt as though it was going to be ours because they screamed these bombs as they came down, and I can remember to this day the sound of it, it was so terrifying. We clung on, our mum and dad put their arms round us and then it got really bad but I think, I think there was about five bombs in a very close area to us and we could hear bricks falling so we knew. On one occasion I remember me father saying "This is ours."*

"I remember me mum saying "Jack, everything you've worked for is gone," cos we thought, the house, part of our house was down, was down on top of us. Not on top of us but in a bad state and it lasted a long, long time. It was really frightening and then eventually the all-clear came and dad went up the cellar steps and he opened the door and all the doors and window frames was gone.

All the greenhouse was obliterated, gone, all the birds had gone. All of it had been blown away with the blast of the bombs that were surrounding us and me dad took, he said to me mum, oh and then we all walked up the cellar steps, mum went upstairs and she said, "Oh look" and I remember looking up and there was a great big hole and we

could see daylight. It came through the attic and it came through the bedroom and it was a massive part of the pavement, I think or something, a massive, massive big piece of stone

"There was a strong, strong smell of burning and dad and I walked down and he said to mum "pack some cases because we can't stay here" and he said "I'll go and see if I can find someone to take us away from here" and of course we were fortunate because me father, well he weren't wealthy but he was, you know, he could afford to pay anyone to take us quickly.

"There was a body part in our front garden but I didn't realise what it was then until afterwards you know, I think me father, more or less, drew me away.

"She got this budgie, Joey, they called it, and it was in a cage that was all bent and it had not got a feather on it. And it was swearing because the people who came to deliver the bread and 'owt like that used to teach it to swear. It was saying "Bugger me, bugger me, bugger me" and it adn't any feathers bless it but it was alive, and I'll never, ever forget the bombs coming down, the screaming, no, cos that's how they sounded."

Connie Bentley:

"When the siren sounded we went to next door's reinforced cellar. Inside were Mr and Mrs Knubley and their son Gordon; Mr and Mrs Frith from the post office, Jimmy, me and my sister, mother and dad and Bruce our dog.

"Mother sat in an armchair with us all around her. Mr Knubley had been into town to see the bombing and to see what was happening. He said 'It's all a-fire in Sheffield. Fire-fighters were being killed. Bombs were dropping all night and air raid wardens kept shouting 'Are you all right?'

"Then we had this terrible shattering of noise and everything shook and everything came tumbling down in the cellar and hit me dad in back of neck.

"We all stood up at once and we got through door to the next cellar, but it was closed because it was the post office and we couldn't get through, so we went upstairs and it were all on fire upstairs. A land mine had dropped on Burgoyne Road and Bloor Street killing thirteen people.

"We had to stay with relatives. When mum and dad went back to the shop it had been robbed."

Pauline Thrones:

"My parents, Percy and Doris Canington, were licencees of the Westminster Hotel, High Street, and we were in the cellars with staff and customers until it caught fire along with Walsh's [department store]. We moved to two more shelters before being taken to The Star offices where we were given cups of tea – this was about 6am. After losing everything at the Westminster Hotel he went to the Grand Hotel and then into the army."

Ivy Heaton:

"I lived on Shoreham Street and worked at Moor & Wrights on the machines making feelers which contributed to the making of bombs and other military equipment needed so desperately for the war effort.

"I was making my way up the Moor as Sheffield was blitzed. I was running to take shelter in The Marples Hotel when a stranger came up to me and asked where I was heading. He took me by the arm and said he knew of a shelter much nearer.

"I owe my life to a complete stranger. The Marples was devastated that night."

Carol Butler:

"My mother often spoke of her brother and sister-in-law, who died during the Blitz. Her brother, Norman Davies, aged 23, worked as a barman in the Marples Hotel. On the night of the Blitz he was working there. His wife, Phyliss, joined him. They both died and their bodies were never found."

Denis Ward:

"I vividly remember the hail of incendiary bombs followed by the stack of high explosives which fell on Woodseats early in the evening. My home was severely damaged by fire and our neighbour's house was completely destroyed. We had to be evacuated."

Mary's story:

"I woke up early on Thursday morning [December 12th] with a big smile on my face. On Saturday I was going to be bridesmaid for my Uncle Joe. He was my mother's youngest brother and he was marrying a girl called Elsie at St. Catherine's Church at Pitsmoor. I had never been a bridesmaid before and my dress was white with pink rosebuds on it. My mother had saved clothing coupons and had managed to save enough to buy me white sandals.

"Today after school I was going to grandma's house, and Elsie was taking me and the other two bridesmaids to have the final fitting of the dresses. Uncle Joe was fetching me from school and would bring me home after the fitting. Half past three took forever, but suddenly it was now and he was here. He swung me in the air and said:

'How's my second best girl?' That was because Elsie was his first best girl. He came to see us often because my daddy was in the Royal Air Force and fighting in North Africa.

"We lived on a new estate on the outskirts of the city. I was six, my brother was five and my sister was three. Uncle Joe wasn't in the army – he worked in a steel mill making shells and bombs.

"We walked together and caught the tramcar into Sheffield, then another tram to Pitsmoor where my grandma lived. She had made a potato pie - no meat just gravy and potatoes. She lived in a large house on the corner of two roads. We had our tea, then Elsie came and we walked to the dressmaker's house. When we were finished the dressmaker said they would be ready for Friday evening and Elsie said she would fetch them when she got home from work. It was half past six and we walked back and Elsie went home. Uncle Joe got our coats and was just ready to take me home when the air raid sirens went. Grandma said to hang on for a while – it probably wasn't going to be much. Within minutes the sound of low planes and explosions not far away.

"'Shelter,' shouted grandma. Uncle Joe looked at me and said, 'Maybe we will get you home later. There were three shelters in the yard. Each house had its own Anderson Shelter. Grandma had made hers very cosy. It had seats around the side, cushions, rugs and blankets. There were games like Ludo and cards, a tin of biscuits, and cups and plates. I'd only ever played in here before. There was also a big statue of Our Lady and a crucifix and few sets of rosary beads.

"The noises outside were loud and I was very frightened. Grandma started saying the rosary and I worried about my mum, brother and sister. Uncle Joe worried about Elsie. Grandma prayed for everyone, calling out their names. The bombing got nearer - you could hear them whistle before they exploded. Everything shook.

"Then the loudest bang I'd ever heard. The shelter shook and became really hot inside. Another explosion then shouting and crying and banging on our shelter door. Mr Pearson from the next shelter wanted to come inside because his had been damaged by shrapnel. His shoulder was bleeding and Mrs Pearson was screaming about her cat. Grandma made some space. She wrapped me in an eiderdown and told me to keep my head down. She gave me rosary beads and holy water. Then I overheard whispering about the Platts from the bottom shelter. Uncle Joe wanted to sneak off to see how Elsie was, in the next street. Grandma said not to go. The noise was terrible and frightening and the smell of burning seeped into the shelter.

"Then we heard my Aunty Mary shouting to us. She drove an ambulance and was nearby, so she'd come to check on us. She said Sheffield was on fire with lots dead and injured. I thought she meant our family – not realizing we were just outside of the city. All night long, bombs fell. I could hear shouts and cries for help. Burning and screaming filled the air. I hid under the eiderdown and cried.

"Morning came slowly, no one had slept. Then the sound we longed for – the all clear. Nobody spoke. Uncle Joe looked out of the shelter at the house. There were no windows left, no doors, the curtains were rags blowing in the December wind. Grandma made the *sign of the cross and went into her home. I had to stay where I was. Nobody wanted to look at the flattened shelter of the Platt family. Uncle Joe wanted to go and check Elsie was alright; she was fine.*

"A fireman came with big jugs of hot water and grandma made some tea. So many houses were gone. Men were scrambling over piles of rubble shouting out names. Uncle Joe said he'd take me home. 'Will they all be dead?' I asked. He cuddled me and said everything would be fine.

"We had to walk. There were no trams. Everyone had dirty faces. There were bodies laying in the street covered by coats. It took us two hours to walk;

sometimes Uncle Joe carried me on his shoulders. As we came along the road my mother came running towards us. She gathered me into her arms and I could feel the tears running down her face onto mine.

"The dressmaker's house was bombed – she was killed and the wedding dresses destroyed. Aunty Elsie borrowed a dress and a fur coat. I wore my best dress but it wasn't a long one with rosebuds on. Everyone tried to have a good time and I wondered if I'd ever get to be a proper bridesmaid. All I really wanted was for this war to be over. I wanted my daddy home and my mummy to stop crying. I am an old lady now but remember that day and night like it was yesterday."

Norman Vincent Price (commonly known as Jim Price):

"I had just ended my shift at Woodhouse and Rixon's steelworks where we were making armaments in the forge. It was December 12th, 1940. It was a moonlit night as I made my way home. The barrage balloons floated high in the sky. These pot-bellied shapes cast an eerie sight as the moon shone down on them. Every building was blacked out. It was bitterly cold and there was little traffic. I got home at six o'clock. My wife was eight and a half months pregnant and baking cakes. My son Peter was playing with his Dinky cars.

"We lived at 11 Court, 4 Woodside Lane. It was a block of four cottages. The houses were divided by a large yard containing eight outside toilets. All four cottages had a front garden with an Anderson Shelter.

"At first we didn't pay too much attention to the sirens. They used to go off two to three times a week. The all-clear hadn't sounded so I decided to put my wife and child in the shelter. It was cold so I lit the Primus Stove to heat the place. As I went back to the house the drone of a plane flying high

could be heard. I thought it was one of ours until I noticed a sparkle of lights appear around Neepsend and I realised it was dropping incendiary bombs to act as flares.

"My wife asked if I'd go back into the house and turn the cakes over. 'I'll go when this one's gone over.' It had just dropped its load on the Gas Works (or so I thought) but it actually dropped its last bomb right in the middle of our yard and blew the houses inside out. We scrambled out and that's when we made our big mistake. We panicked and went looking for another shelter. Sheffield was a blazing mass. "German fighter bombers were firing tracer bullets at barrage balloons. I was crawling over rubble clutching my son to my chest. Doris was following with bullets flying all around. We really thought the world was coming to an end. Flames were shooting sixty foot high out of the Gas Works.

"Air raid wardens led us to a chapel halfway up Woodside which was packed with people. We would have been better off staying in our shelter which was steel and untouched. We stood in the archway of the chapel for at least two hours watching Sheffield being blown to bits."

Brian Clayton:

"I was four-years-old in the Blitz and was living with my mother at Rodley Lane (off Bramall Lane). Even now I can remember being in the cellar with the neighbours when it received a direct hit. Everything was black and people were screaming. I was carried out by a fireman (they couldn't find my mother and I was taken to Greystones School where we were eventually reunited – she was hysterical). Many of the neighbours in the cellar didn't make it. I can remember returning to see what was left of our house. I can still hear mum's screams to this day as she said, 'Look Brian, they're taking our bloody table.' Two burly men were carrying our table up the lane. Nothing else was left. We were re-housed temporarily on Hawley Street."

Death at The Marples Hotel

by Alan Turner

The London Mart, Fitzallan Square, was known locally as Marples, after the Marples family who owned it.

The hotel was seven stories high and had guest bedrooms, music and concert rooms, bars and lounges with a vast array of cellars. It was considered at the time to be a safe building. It stood on the corner of Fitzallen Square and next door was a nurseryman shop owed by Fisher Son and Sibray Ltd

On the night of the German bombing raid on Sheffield, December 12th, 1940, it was a clear and cold night. People headed into town for a drink - many made their way to the Marples, which was very popular.

The air raid siren was sounded at 7pm. At around 10.50pm the C&A Modes building across the road from the hotel took a direct hit and blew some of the windows out at the hotel. People injured in these rooms were cared for by the staff, who ushered them down stairs into the cellars for safety. At 11.44pm the hotel took a direct hit and collapsed like a pack of cards. The weight of the rubble caused the cellar roof to collapse. Over 70 people died. There are still bodies buried there.

King George and Queen Elizabeth visited Sheffield the next day. Many stories have been written about this event, many names have been discovered from the archives. Here is my list of the dead and of the survivors.

Those that died

Ethel Beardshaw *née Dodd*	27	Joiner's bench hand	20 Fowler Terrace
Dorothy Brisbane	42	Variety artist	43 Broomgrove Rd, Sheffield
Robert Brisbane	40	Variety artist	43 Broomgrove Rd, Sheffield
Arthur Brewer	33	Lorry driver	34 Thornhill, Dewsbury
Francis Brown	70	Pensioner	86 Fairfax Road, Sheffield
Arthur Clarence Burgess	46	Manager of the Marples Hotel	196 Bradway Road, Sheffield
Alfred Butcher	49		
Ada Buxton *née Jackson*	35	French polisher	144 Sutherland Road
George Frederick William Carpenter	58		Dovedale Ave, Ilford, Essex
Evelyn Carr *née Lawless*	36	Warehouse clerk	32 Southey Drive, Sheffield
Edith Charles	51		Broom Lane, Rotherham
Jess Cockayne	43	Lorry Driver	Nottinghamshire
Harold Cooper	46	Chief Commissionaire	19 Thorpe House Ave, Sheffield
Winifred Dalby *née Young*	35	Barmaid/waitress	34 Southey Drive, Sheffield
Norman Plaxton Davis	23	Barman	Sheffield
Phyllis Davis	22		Summer St, Sheffield
Mabel Dean *née Siddall*	30	Waitress	14 Kimberley St, Sheffield
Frederick TC Dixon	59	Musician	20 Barncliffe Rd
Margaret M Ebbatson	39	Barmaid/waitress.	Chesterfield Rd, Sheffield
James Fletcher	34	Railway porter	51 Kent Rd, Heeley, Sheffield
Lily Fletcher	32		Main Rd, Sheffield
Edith Annie Guess *née Westby*	29		Lund Rd, Sheffield
Henry Hattersley	63	Spring knife cutler	Cookswood Close, Sheffield
John H Hoggins	30	Bricklayer's labourer	Staffordshire

Arnold Victor Jenkinson	25		2 Hunter House Road, Sheffield
Edna May Ahmed Khan	22		Filey St, Sheffield
William Kirby	57	Metal sawyer	99 Dagnam Rd, Sheffield
Florence Longden *née Wathall*	25	Waitress/barmaid	212 London Rd, Sheffield
Joseph Clifford Marsden	66	Builder/labourer	16 Machon Bank Rd, Sheffield
Ruth Ellen Morris	26		27 Fawley Rd, Sheffield
Ernest Peace	33	Colliery lamp man	West Ave, Rawmarsh, Rotherham
Ezra Peace	49	Club steward	313 Sheffield Rd, Sheffield
Noreen Rackham *née Knight*	23	Waitress/licensed victualler	2 Broomhall St, Sheffield
Henry V Raynor	47	Machine shop foreman	45 St Nicolas Rd, Rawmarsh, Rotherham
Bernard Douglass Roe	22		18 Nethergreen, Sheffield
Madge Smith	24		112 Basford St, Sheffield
Harry Sansom	32		
Lilian Shooter *née Dodd*		Barmaid/waitress	4 Dawlish Close, Sheffield
Elsie Siddall	45		144 Sutherland Road, Sheffield
Charles Fred Smith	51		Leppings Lane, Sheffield
Irene Steel *née Oxspring*	26	Waitress /barmaid	Bellhouse Rd, Sheffield
George Taylor	42		Chesterfield Road, Sheffield
Lily Taylor	46	Barmaid /waitress	45 Holme Lane Hillsborough Sheffield Single born 13th October 1894
Gertrude Thorpe *née Bacon*	27		Abbeydale Road, Sheffield
William Travers	51	Steelworks labourer	Normandale Rd, Sheffield
William Walker	29	Steelworker	Penisone Rd, Sheffield
Albert Wallace	31	Drop forge worker	Fawley St, Sheffield
Eva Westby	34		Southey Drive, Sheffield
Elizabeth Wildsmith	38	Barmaid/waitress	Fulton Rd, Sheffield
Edith Grace Wilson	30	Barmaid /Waitress	Bastock Rd, Sheffield

The survivors

William Wallace King	29	Transport Motor Driver.	Albert Parade, Bristol
Lionel George Ball	26		Knowle West, Bristol.
Ebenezer T Tall	42	Export packing clerk	Hackney, London.
Edward Riley	36	Cellerman at The Banner Cross Hotel, Banner Cross, Sheffield.	
John Watson Keay	44	Co-Op Insurance agent and a Volunteer Ambulance Driver.	46 Boma Road, Trentham Stoke.

Seven people reportedly survived the Marples bombing. We say 'reported' as Blitz fireman Doug Lightning said no one lived to tell the tale – he says the seven actually emerged from an air raid shelter next door. It's unlikely we'll ever know for sure. But for the purpose of this book we are listing the people that were reported at the time as having survived.

Two of them refused to give their names when they were rescued. One was reported to have committed suicide within two years having struggled for 24 months with what he witnessed that night.

It is believed the other man could have been Benjamin Wilkinson of 61 Sorby Street Pitsmoor, Sheffield.

My brother-in-law, Eric Stinson, said that he was told by his mother, Ivy Stinson née Welton, sister of Lily Wilkinson wife of Ben, that Ben was in the Marples pub on the night of the Blitz and was rescued the following morning. He later developed MS and died in 1956.

The following were all military, army or R.A.F. and killed in the Marples bombing.

Albert James Abbott	Royal Artillary	Number 983721	
Alfred Butterworth	Royal Artillary	Number 1648060	Born London
Duncan Kerr Howie	Royal Artillary	Number 1567022	Born Stirling Scotland
C Hurley	Royal Artillary		Regimental Number wrongly recorded – information missing
Derek Douglas Millard	Royal Artillary	Number 915439	Born Bedford
Albert Buckley Ogden	Royal Artillary Lance Bombardier	Number 1496983	Born Manchester
Joseph Smith	Royal Artillary Gunner	Number 1567125	Born Dumfriesshire
Sylvester Swan	Royal Artillary Private	75 Anti Aircraft Battery	
Edward Maddock	Royal Artillary Gunner	Number 1640169	Born Toxteth Liverpool 1909
Frank Dalton	R.A.F.	Number 937424	Age 29 Aircraftman 2 class 16 Balloon Centre. Frank Dalton looked to be from Sheffield
James G.Forbes	R.A.F.	Number 1109587	Age 35 New Elgin Bar Elgin Glasgow Aircraftman 2 class 16 Balloon Centre
Thomas Jones	R.A.F.	Number 1021753	Age 28 Howards House Andrews lane Formby Liverpool. Occupation 1939 was Travelling Sales Manager Transport Driver. His all family were involved in transport Aircraftman 2 class 16 Balloon Centre
William C. Mcdonald	R.A.F.	Number 1670559	Age 31 32 Middlesex St High Brox Glasgow. Aircraftman 2 class 16 Balloon Centre
Frank Mchugh	R.A.F	Number 1108092	Age 32 38 High Street Wavertree Liverpool. Aircraftman 2 class 16 Balloon Centre

Above: The Marples Hotel rescue.
Right: Attending to a Marples Hotel survivor.

My memories when I was a five-year-old child in 1939

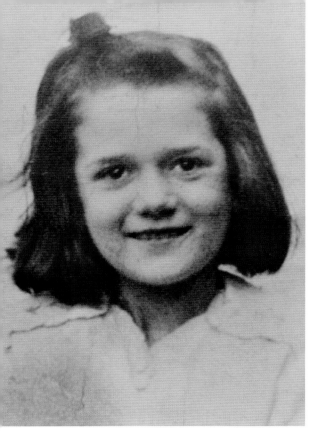

Mabel Lucy Willoughby.

I was five when war started. It was very exciting getting up in the middle of the night and putting my siren suit on and going outside into the air raid shelter in the back yard. Mother would take a stone hot water bottle and brown paper carrier bag with what I called 'goodies' in it. These would be broken biscuits, colouring book and crayons.

One day a battalion of soldiers marched up our road of terraced houses and the sergeant knocked on certain doors and soldiers were billeted there. All the children on our road were hoping to have one!

Two were billeted in our yard and one of these – Donald – used to send me letters and postcards. I thought of him as my soldier sweetheart!

I remember these were happy days as our mother shielded us from the sad or bad war news.

All the children on our road went to someone's house for school lessons.

I remember the war being over and being very disappointed. I wanted to go into the ATS like my elder sister. I asked my mum to write to Mr Churchill about the war finishing too early – she used to say she would just to pacify me!

Barrage balloons over Sheffield

The deployment of barrage balloons in and around Sheffield was coordinated from an office on Bridge St, that was a former confectionery business. This was used until they moved command to Norton Lightwood Lane. Several personnel were killed during the Sheffield Blitz of 12th December whilst on a night off. I suggest those above fit the bill for those killed.

How they were deployed usually by a winch fasted to several blocks or a truck.

The following day stunned helpers on the site of the 15-foot pile of rubble were amazed to see that a flight of steps had been exposed. On further inspection several people- seven in total - had survived and they were helped out to safety.

Nurse Edna attends to the wounded

Frank Donnelly of South Yorkshire Aircraft Museum, sent in the story of a nurse who worked in Sheffield during the Blitz. In 1940, Edna Sherwin, whose family home was in Chesterfield, was an 18-year-old student nurse, working at the Sheffield Royal Hospital on West Street in the city centre. The nurses lived at Tapton Court Nurses' Home at Fulwood, about two miles from the hospital. The working day for the nurses was a long one, from 8am to 8pm. They got a half-day off per week, a half-day off every other Sunday, and a full day off a month. They could, by arrangement, also take two hours off in the morning or evening to get shopping done, etc. They were paid 28 shillings a month (£1.40). The Blitz night, Thursday December 12th, was Edna's night off, having worked from 8am. They could eat in the hospital but were mostly served pasta. Pasta! Leaving the hospital at 6pm with three other young nurses, they went to the Fleur de Lys cafe for tea, which was upstairs on Division Street. For 9d they could have beans or egg on toast, and for 1d extra they could have a bun or a cup of tea. Just as they were finishing their meal, about 7pm, two uniformed sailors rushed in, shouting: "They're dropping flares" and flares were lighting up the sky like a bonfire party. This was the start of the air raid by German bombers. Edna and her colleagues rushed back to the hospital for safety. The afternoon staff had gone home and the evening staff were in working. Edna and her colleagues got 'collared' for another 12-hour shift, where they worked all night. Beside the old hospital was a new three-storey building, provided by the Miners' Welfare. The operating theatres were on the top floor. The first thing that happened was a big bang from an exploding high-explosive bomb close by, which shattered all the windows in the operating theatres, and all the lights went out. The nursing staff immediately started to evacuate the patients from the second floor, down to the basement. Anybody who could walk, walked down the stairs. Those patients on traction had their strings cut and were helped to lie on the floor until they could be moved downstairs with the help of the porters. Ambulances and fire engines were running about all night. All the staff could hear were big bangs from exploding bombs all around them. One elderly patient wouldn't leave without their hat! "Where's my hat? I can't leave without my hat!" she called. All the patients were eventually taken down to basement level, where the staff opened the cellars, and were shocked to discover huge quantities of coffins in storage for the anticipated emergency situation as necessary. For Edna and her fellow colleagues, emerging from the hospital that morning was a stunning shock. The hospital stood, surrounded by almost complete devastation- shops and houses totally shattered, buses and trams wrecked and burning. The city centre was almost completely destroyed. As there was no transport running, the nurses walked up to Fulwood for a wash, rest and food, before being called back to the hospital in the afternoon. They had to walk miles further to avoid unexploded bombs which were all over the place. The hospital had lost its water supply, so it was necessary to extract water from the swimming baths on Glossop Road. One of the major tragedies of that terrible night was the direct hit on the five-storey Marples Hotel, killing 77 people. Only seven people survived and only 14 bodies were identified. Edna said the search and recovery lasted for almost two weeks. How the Sheffield Royal Hospital survived the bombing can only be described as miraculous. The following Sunday, December 15th, Edna tried to get home to Chesterfield. Her father used to buy her a return bus ticket, so Edna could always get home if she needed to. However, the buses weren't running in Sheffield but Edna and a friend heard that a bus was going from Chesterfield to Meadowhead, four miles away, but when they got there on foot, no bus! Whilst they pondered what to do, a gentleman noticed the two girls in nurses' uniform at the side of the road. He stopped and offered them a lift to Chesterfield, saying that if they were outside a certain cinema at 6pm, he would give them a lift back to Sheffield, their return trip. This had been the first opportunity for Edna to see and reassure her parents that she was alive and well and had survived, when so many had been killed and injured. Few had access to telephones in those days. Edna's parents didn't want her to return to Sheffield because of the danger (Edna's father, understandably, wanted to know who this man was who was offering his daughter a lift back to Sheffield) but Edna said she had to return to continue her training and to do her bit for the country, like her father in a reserved occupation as a miner was doing. When Edna returned to Sheffield that evening, so did the German bombers, who carried out a second air raid, but this time aiming their bombs more at the industrial East End of the city. There were many fatalities as a result of this attack, but not as destructive as the first night. All people could do was put up with the occasional air raids and hope that they lived to tell the tale. Edna survived, God bless her, and went on to have a happy and successful career in nursing, serving her community.

'Blood tub' driver Emma did her bit

A former Sheffielder who vividly remembers the nights of the Blitz in December 1940 is Emma Pyecroft. Aged 18 then, she worked as a driver for the ARP ambulance brigade in Sheffield. "We used to call them the blood tubs," she said. Emma, who lived in Gleadless with her family during the war, gave up a career in the theatre to 'do her bit.'

She said: "I was a ballet dancer and I was in the theatre most of my adult life. About two years into the war, we decided we should do something for the country. I went back to Sheffield and joined the ARP ambulance service.

"It was the blackout and we had to drive with no lights on and no lights in the streets. We were stationed at Carbrook School."

The nights of the first air raids were unforgettable for the young ambulance driver.

She said: "I remember two very big raids on the East End of Sheffield, it was the steelworks they were after, and the one in the centre of Sheffield.

"I remember a whole family that was bombed. They had gone into the air raid shelter and each one we kept bringing out was dead. I remember vividly the last one brought out was a woman with a blue coat with a big black fur collar. I picked up her foot, which had blown off, and put it with her.

"We had eight bodies in the ambulance and we couldn't find a morgue anywhere. We saw a barn in a field and I said, 'Probably that's a morgue. We carried eight dead bodies over two fields into the barn."

Pretty gruesome stuff for an 18-year-old to cope with but Emma just said: "It was all a part of life's pattern. I was only very young. When you're young, you cope with anything."

Emma recalled the scene that night

as she drove through the city streets: "It was all on fire and burned. It was terrible, there were fires burning all over and people in the air raid shelters. As soon as the sirens would go you had to go straight on duty, so I walked to Carbook School with the bombs dropping. A big lorry came down and drove me straight down to the school, where I went on duty."

Emma used her theatre skills to do her bit for morale, too. "I organised a concert at Carbrook School with ambulance staff. We called it Blitz and Pieces. People came in and watched it, so it provided a bit of entertainment." She also danced solo to entertain wounded soldiers.

Memorable Blitz night for Telegraph boy Ken

Memories of the worst night of the Sheffield Blitz on December 12th, 1940 came flooding back for wartime telegram boy, Ken Foster. He was in Sheffield city centre when the worst of the bombing started, and narrowly avoided being one of the victims in the Marples Hotel. He and another telegram boy, Albert Land, had been to night school on Queen Street, which was compulsory for them. Ken joined the telegram service at the beginning of the war when he was 14.

He said: "We left at 9pm. The teacher said that we shouldn't leave. We made our way on to High Street. Two tram cars were still standing there and we heard a noise like heavy rain. It was the noise of shrapnel raining down.

"The two of us got on this tram and, when the noise stopped, we made our way to Fitzalan Square. As we went past the Marples Hotel, a man came to the door. He called out right rudely, 'You

two ruffians, come in here and shelter'. We ignored it. I'm glad we did as they were all killed.

"We'd go from shelter to shelter. There was one that was in Pond Hill. We stayed there the rest of the night."

The shelter was built from bricks and sandbags and stood near Pond Street bus station and was for transport workers, said Ken. He remembers: "Someone said, 'get in here, you two'." When he finally made his way home, he found his parents waiting anxiously on the corner for him.

Ken said: "It was a remarkable thing the next day. There were about 40 telegram boys in those days and they all turned up for work. The bombs had damaged the electronics network and telegrams had to be sent to Leeds and brought to Sheffield by van and on foot."

He remembered that telegrams wouldn't arrive until 1pm and then the telegram boys would all disappear off in different directions with their deliveries.

"The following few days we climbing over destroyed buildings. The telegrams were the only communications from the outside world at that point. People were sending telegrams asking, 'are you alright?' When we got to certain houses they were demolished."

Sometimes the telegram boys were able to get a new address off neighbours for the people whose homes had been burned out. And other times, of course, the houses had been hit by tragedy. Ken said that, as a youngster, he coped surprisingly well with delivering bad news.

"As time went on we just adjusted to the war. We had our jobs to do. We only had eight days annual leave and worked quite late at night.

"There was a togetherness that will never come again. We were a vital part of the war effort." Ken, who is now 90 and lives near Trowbridge in Wiltshire, lived with his family in Heeley during the war. He says he is still a Wednesdayite! He had been a pupil at Woodseats School but only got his school certificate after completing night school.

Ken wonders how many of the city's wartime telegram boys are left alive now: "We never had a reunion or get-together. One or two went in the RAF. I went into the Navy on the Atlantic convoys and served on a destroyer.

Some telegram boys were killed in the war.

"It would be lovely to find out. We were just boys. They didn't have telegram girls but girls aged 14 to 15 were called girl probationers, dealing with all the telegram traffic coming in."

Ken served in the Atlantic convoys on the destroyer HMS Viceroy as a wireless operator and then went out to the Pacific on the HMS Anson. The Viceroy sank two U-boats — and the crew recovered a canister containing bottles of schnapps from the wreckage. The captain decided to send a presentation case of part of the find to Churchill and Ken got a copy of the letter of thanks that he sent back. He has kindly supplied a copy of it to Retro. Apparently he never enjoyed a nip of the hard stuff, though.

He said he was never scared during his time in the Navy: "I am amazed now. At the time I was 17 or 18 and at sea. But that's why young men can go to Afghanistan. You think, 'how did they put up with that lot?' and it's because they were young.

"I got my war medals from the Navy but I didn't get anything for being a telegram boy. I didn't expect anything."

A gripping account of the first night of the Blitz written by George Hennings, a watchman at Roberts Brothers store on the Moor, came via his granddaughter, Jean McLoughlin, from Kiveton Park.

"Somehow, it seemed as if there was something ominous in the very air and I remarked to the men who assisted me: "I think we are in for a bad spell of trouble. Get you down to the air raid shelter!" I counselled the men to stay there while I went round to turn off all electric light and gas at the main. Soon after this, there was a terrific noise and I was apprehensive of great danger. Time passed quickly. It had now got to 8pm and I went to the roof in search of incendiary bombs. This I had to do alone, for those with me were terror-stricken. From the roof I could see many fires. Near this very spot- at the top of Matilda Street- Wilson's the wholesale tobacconist's shop was well alight.

"Looking up Pinstone Street I could see Campbell's furniture stores was a blazing mass, flames leaping many feet high. About this hour I took a group of firemen some hot milk, for they were nearly frozen. It was so bitterly cold. Then we were informed that water was scarce and shortly afterwards it went off altogether for the night. What a tragedy! Going on to the roof again, I could see flames all around- Heeley, Millhouses, Abbeydale- what a position! Here was I, helpless as a child, unable to do a thing to avert disaster which I felt sure would befall the very place I was in.

"Down below, my men were wandering around demented with fear. I realised they could only be a hindrance to me and by no means a help, so I bade them to go home. This they ventured to do, only to find that in some instances their homes had been blasted and destroyed by bombs and fire. Going to the shop front about 9.30pm, I looked down the Moor and saw to my horror many shops and trams ablaze. Then I realised what a Blitz meant to us in Sheffield. At this time there was little wind stirring and the fires were confined to the bottom part of the Moor. I could hear bombs falling in the distance, and see fires starting in many more districts. Back I went to the roof of our own store, to remain there until midnight. Then I realised that I could feel in no way safe at such a height, with the possibility of every avenue of escape cut off. Just at this time. I was hit by a piece of shrapnel. It must have been from a shell bursting in the air near to our building. A coping stone bore marked evidence of this, for about two feet of stone was chipped out. Fortunately for me, I wore my steel helmet. The only effect the shrapnel had upon me was a dint in the helmet and the sensation of shock to the head with the sharp impact of steel upon the helmet. To say I was grateful is an altogether too mild expression.

"At about 10.30pm, a great change took place- bombs fell (both fire bombs and explosive bombs) everywhere, or so it seemed. Everybody was in a state of excitement and by this time the flames were creeping up the Moor. A strong wind rose at this hour and fanned the blaze into something like fury. Debris was falling all around and our store got its first shock as I stood in the Arcade. A great tremor caused by a bomb exploding near blasted out our great windows. Glass and woodwork were flying around us like hail in a whirling storm.

" Happily I escaped with just a few minor injuries which a drop of iodine relieved for the moment. The wind came up from the Moor with a great force- like a hurricane, helping the flames along; and yet it was bitterly cold. All the buildings, by midnight, were ablaze- Atkinson's, Darley's, Gebhart's, Langton's and many others. I, along with others, could only wait in fear and trembling, wondering as to what would be our fate.

"There was a great ominous, rumbling noise. Another bomb dropped near and, looking round, I saw to my surprise that the back of the parcel office and all the stairs had collapsed from the effect of a bomb, which crashed near the bottom of Rockingham Street. This caused much havoc in the neighbourhood. From this time onwards, bombs of every type seemed to fall continuously. Standing outside, close to our store, I saw many things happen round about me which made one feel anything but brave, and yet, like a lad in the last war, I was "afraid of being afraid". It was all so frightful, so fiendishly indescribable.; firemen, ambulancemen, ARP wardens and workers, and all branches of civil defence were all doing their bit and doing it well.

"Many people were trapped in shelters under shops.; sulphur and burning material made these untenable, and still everyone stuck to the job in hand, while destruction played its fiendish part. At about 2am a very old man came to me and asked me if I was interested in any firm, as he thought I might be Robert's watchman. He had seen a man similar to me at different periods. He told me he was the watchman at Woolworth's and that while he was sitting in the cellar, a bomb about the size of a fire extinguisher came through the shop floor into the cellar.

 He coolly said: "I knelt down to examine it and heard something ticking inside so thought I had better come out of their premises." Woolworth's blew up at 2.30am! The bomb was a time bomb! If I had not advised the man to stay out, he would have gone back. The Moor up Rockingham Street was well alight. Atkinson's burning furiously. I stood at the top of Matilda Street and wondered what would be the outcome. Near to me, a fireman had been blown across the road. When found, he was badly wounded, his leg had been blown off. For six months he was in hospital. He is now employed in the Fire Office as a telephone operator. He has been fitted with an aluminium leg. The landlord of the Monument Tavern, situated near to our staff entrance, was talking to me at 3.30am, having just come out of the cellar. Back of Button Lane, on our side, was alright at this period. Shortly after, what a change! Fletcher's furniture works, Bingham's and Warmby's, Neville and sons, all going up in smoke at one time. And yet, there was no sign of serious damage to our store. I walked round whenever I could, hoping for the best. Fear had left me, and a peculiar unafraid mentality took possession of me. News of disaster passed on from one part of the city to the other from time to time, and still there was no chance of water to extinguish the fires raging in the surrounding buildings. It was now dangerous to be in the open for debris and shrapnel was flying in all directions. The Moor was one huge mass of flames. Right and left, in most parts, gas mains and electric mains were torn up.

"Above our store, at 3.45am, Bray's and Binn's and the rest of the shops on Button Lane were well alight, starting one after the other. Redgate's, part of Berry's Vaults, Woolworth's, the Devonshire and other places, were going one after the other in explosion and flame. Rats and cats were fleeing in all directions, but never did I see a dog the whole night through. Then our fate gradually drew nearer. Material in flames was flying up the Moor, helped by a wind like a hurricane. This blew through every open window- and still we were unscathed.

"Just before 4am, a sergeant-fireman and I were standing by Burton's the Tailors, looking up to our roof opposite. We both saw small fires starting in the mantle and dressmaking workroom. We rushed across and for a time fought the flames with all the means at our disposal- extinguishers, sand, any water available- and succeeded in getting the fires out. Soon after 4am, we turned downstairs to see what else we could do. Looking through the mantle department, we saw the extreme end of the store, the millinery department and all that end, was enveloped in flames. We could do no more, for the heat was so intense and the smoke was suffocating. We could only come out into the open, to watch from the other side. In 10 minutes, the whole building was one mass of flames. Fifty or more firemen were waiting to do their duty but they were helpless- no water!

"Then, about this time, the 'all-clear' sounded. Our building went on burning. Many people were released from shelters in and around our district in the Moor area- 130 lost their lives about here. As one moved about the neighbourhood, one would be startled by a voice from a damaged shelter, or a cellar grate, asking if the 'all-clear' had sounded. And oh, what strange sights greeted our eyes everywhere; men and women, blackened with soot, smoke and powder blast. Destruction, devastation everywhere. and, by God's grace, here we were - spared!"

Frank Yates – Royal Artillery Light Anti-Aircraft Regiments

"My leave ended on December 12th, a date fixed in my memory. I caught the 18.45 train to Manchester, from Sheffield Victoria station. While waiting for the train, the 'red' warning sounded and, as we were about to leave, the station announcer gave the 'purple' warning, and even the heavily shaded lights were turned off in the train. The train was crowded and as the differential between first and second-class compartments had disappeared, I found myself sitting next to a lieutenant from Rotherham. He was also going back to Saighton, and we walked back to the camp together, admiring the night sky, on a bitterly cold, brilliantly clear night,

"So the training went on, with Major Hardy taking a great interest in everything going on. He had us over to the rifle range at nearby Eaton Hall, where again, I found the problem of being strongly left-eyed, although a better shot than most, meant that the standard Lee Enfield rifle, when fired from the left shoulder, made the manipulation of the bolt most awkward.

"I also had a problem, known about since my Boy Scout Marksman badge, that when lying down in the approved prone position, with legs spread, I was, and still am, unable to turn my heels flat to the ground. I have had several arguments with instructors, pointing out that, if the object of the exercise is to kill the enemy, my physical deviations from the norm have no significance. As I was usually a better shot than most, I won my argument. Major, Hardy, never without his WW1, nickel plated Webley revolver, could not resist having a 'pot' at the 25-yard range, and even let some of the NCOs have a go, challenging us to even hit the target! A big pistol, fired one-handed, kicks upward, on recoil, and misses the target. The answer is to hold the weapon two-handed, as in the modern TV 'cop' films. As a matter of interest, when I had my own Webley, a couple of years later, I found that the only way to hit the middle of the target, was to sit down on the ground, facing the target, pressing the barrel of the pistol hard into the groove between my knees, to steady it. Don't believe the shooting skills of the Hollywood cowboys!

"On the evening of the 20th December, a week after returning from leave, I glanced at a newspaper in the Sgts' mess and saw the headline "SHEFFIELD BLITZED." I, of course, was very worried about the family, but received a letter, next morning from my sister Gladys, reassuring me that they were okay, but our house had lost some windows and the kitchen ceiling, and Mum was safely living with her in Reservoir Road until the repairs had been done.

"Wartime security had delayed the release of the news and I discovered that the Blitz had been, in fact, on the night of the 12th, and the first bomb had fallen, through the Wicker Arches, 15 minutes after my train had crossed it. I often think about that pleasant walk to Saighton Camp on that lovely starlit night, chatting with my Rotherham friend, completely oblivious to the devastation that was taking place back home."

John Unsworth:

"Many people died because they had relied on air raid shelters under buildings that received direct hits."

The Blitz through the eyes of an 11 year old

A Sheffielder who lost his home, his father and brother in the Sheffield Blitz has told his story of the terrible night that changed his family forever.

Harry Kenny was just 11 years old when a German landmine exploded outside his house in Musgrave Crescent, Shirecliffe.

Harry tells how most of the family were in their home on the night of the raid because their Anderson shelter was unfinished. They were joined by two elderly women who lived next door and were frightened by the bomb blasts.

"The guns started firing straightaway and bombs were dropping and we knew then that this was no ordinary raid. It was our turn to be blitzed."

Harry's father, Sylvester, aged 47, was in the back garden fire-watching, his sister Edith, aged 18, was sheltering under the table with Harry and the old ladies.

Brother Vin, aged 16, was asleep on the sofa after a shift at a steelworks.

His mum Alice, aged 44, was cooking supper on the fire for an older son, Tom aged 23, who was working a 2-10 shift at a steelworks.

Younger sons Billy, 14, and Walt, eight, were also in the house while Joe, aged 20, was at the cinema.

Harry described the moment that the landmine exploded outside while he was sheltering under the kitchen table.

Just before that, he and his father had been watching the Germans dropping flares to light up their targets.

Harry said: "I went inside and I went under the kitchen table and then the next minute it was a big red, green and yellow flash and I saw the back door come off its hinges.

"It was going to hit me in the face when it all smashed up into little bits of wood and the next second it was buried under bricks and mortar.

"The house was absolutely flat. I got out straightaway. It was 10.45pm when we got bombed.

"I got my sister out. I was only a little lad but I was just lifting all these big bricks up and throwing them around."

He was surrounded by a scene of devastation with flames leaping 200 feet into the air from their cul-de-sac.

Harry, who was unhurt, also managed to get the two neighbours out, but he and his sister couldn't reach anybody else and thought they must be dead.

A policeman arrived and helped them to safety and they were taken to the Northern General Hospital (then the City General) in an ambulance driven by a teenage girl.

Harry said: "We went into the casualty. I hadn't got a mark on me. When we were sat there, the doctors were operating on tables just in front of us and I saw a soldier come in with his head blown off. There were people with arms and legs blown off coming in too."

They were moved to stay the night with a group of other casualties in the old Fir Vale workhouse, but got out through a window and walked to their grandad's house. Elder brother Tom arrived after them, having got home from work to see the entire street flattened. He thought everyone had died. Harry and Tom then set off to tour the city's hospitals and morgues to discover what had happened to the rest of their family. Their first find was grim: Harry had to identify the body of Billy, whose bones were shattered. Vin, who had been asleep, was buried deep in the rubble. He was knocked unconscious but was otherwise unhurt and luckily came round just as the search for further bodies was about to be abandoned by the ARP warden. Walt suffered two black eyes and a shoulder injury. Their

father's body wasn't discovered for a week. Harry said that he was unmarked but all his clothes were blown off and the blast had burst his lungs. His mother spent 13 months in hospital and the family had an anxious time waiting to see if she would recover. Alice was blinded by the explosion and glass had lacerated the back of her head and body. She was so badly injured that doctors waited 13 months to tell her she had lost her husband and son. Hospital staff had to waive the usual rules about children visiting to reassure Alice that her younger children had survived. The family had to be moved to a new home in Southey Green. Harry described how their only furniture was a donated barber's chair and a damaged settee, plus some candles. Sadly, the family suffered another loss in 1944 when Edith, who never recovered from that night, died as a result of illness caused by the ordeal.

Thanks to Harry's son, Steve Kenny, for allowing us to tell his late dad's story.

CHAPTER 6

The relief effort
December 13th, 1940

The all-clear rang out at 4.17am. The city was in ruins. Much of it was on fire. Fire crews from miles around were still battling with hundreds of fires. It was chaos. Death and destruction was everywhere.

Friday, 13th Dec

Hardly anything left of Sheffield City and suburbs with the exception of East end and I could cry. I walked nearly all the way to work. Wrecked shop and phone bell ringing inside – smashed cars, tram wires like ropes, on the roads. Twisted irons smashed motors. Wicker Arches with a hole right through. No work today, no light, water, heat at the Office.

Joyce helps co-ordinating the relief effort

Joyce Spurr spent the first night of the Sheffield Blitz in the Library Theatre, under Central Library. She didn't realise, until the following morning, just how lucky they'd been- a huge crater containing an unexploded bomb was on the junction of Surrey Street and Tudor Street, just yards away from the library.

Just how the city's bombed out population would have fared if the bomb had gone off we'll never know; the library spent the following day (and weeks after) helping coordinate the relief effort via its information service, which had been geared to assisting such an event.

She said: "I was working in the Reference Library as a junior assistant, when the alarm sounded at about 7.30pm (we closed at 9pm in those days).

"We were always expecting something to happen as it had been happening in London and places like that.

"We led the public down to the Library Theatre, which was sandbagged as an official shelter. It was absolutely full but people still kept coming in. Me and one of the janitors had to keep going upstairs to make sure that no incendiary bombs had taken hold on the upper floors. There were frightening crashes and bangs, and the building shook. Some of the noise was from anti-aircraft guns. The sky outside was red from the fires of the burning buildings.

"During the evening, some people came in covered in dust and debris. They had come from the evening classes in the College of Art in Arundel Street nearby. It had received a direct hit from a shell and was completely demolished, which was a great pity as it had been an ornate Victorian building with classical sculptures on the facade.

"When the 'all clear' sounded, and we came out, the Air Raid Wardens directed us around a huge crater in which was an unexploded bomb. It was at the corner of Surrey Street and Tudor Street, just alongside the corner of the library, so we had a lucky escape.

"I had to walk home to Woodseats. When I saw The Moor, I was appalled, as it was a blazing inferno with the black skeletons of trams silhouetted against the flames. There were lumps of debris and cables hanging down. It made such a vivid impression on me that the image remained with me for the rest of my life.

"I passed over many fires and saw a notably huge one at Laver's Timber Yard on Queen's Road.

"I remember wondering if I'd have any parents and any house when I got home. Fortunately they'd not been hit.

"My parents were of, course, relieved to see me, but I knew I had to be back at work by 8am, so I only had two hours rest on the settee before walking back to the library. There were no trams or buses of course. The buses started to appear several days later.

"There were still a lot of flames coming out of buildings on The Moor the following day.

"The library had become a gigantic information bureau- I was very impressed about how well-organised they were. Representatives of different parts of the Town Hall sat at desks in the Reference Library to deal with problems of people who had been bombed out and had nowhere to live, or no gas, electricity or water supply, or needed roofs repairing. Desks had little tags on, telling people which issue they could sort out, whether it be no gas, bombed out or whatever.

"Instead of people having to trail round the Town Hall, it was all there at once. The Central Library was the city's information service.

"But it was quite distressing the next morning as people were coming in. In fact an acquaintance of mine came in whilst I had the job of directing everyone. He said: "My wife and son have just been killed- the house got a direct hit." He'd got no home, no family and nowhere to go. There must have been lots of stories like that.

"I do remember how in control everybody seemed to be. I only remember one woman who was moaning and crying and wasn't in control. Somebody said: 'I've got some brandy, I'll give her a tot.' She was a bit better after that. People were quite calm generally. I suppose it was because we were expecting the attacks and we thought: 'We're not going to let those damn Germans get us down.' We were proud of our steel industry, our cutlery and everything else Sheffield was unique in the world for then.

"The Newspaper Room and Children's Library were receiving people who had been bombed out, and the staff kitchen was serving tea, soup and sandwiches to them all day. The police took over the Cataloguing Department and the Library

staff compiled records of the missing and dead people as the information came in. My job was to divert people to the appropriate place for their problems.

"I think this operation went on at least two or three weeks. I also remember it was very cold weather and I had chilblains all over my fingers and I ended up having to have them bandaged up.

"It had been well planned and organised to come into operation immediately and credit, for a large part, must go to the City Librarian, Mr J.P. Lamb.

"It's an experience I'll never forget."

Below: The remains of Atkinsons department store after the Blitz.

Damage to the Empire Theatre, corner of Charles and Union streets.

Mrs S. Lambert:

"When the clearance started they found my auntie's arm with her glove on. It was a three-quarter size and it had her name and address inside. She was taken to City Road Cemetery with others and put in the communal grave.

"I believe she'd gone to the Electra Picture House. When the sirens went off she ran to The Marples Hotel Shelter.

Mrs K. Toulson:

"When we came out of our air raid shelter in the garden my mother went into the house and sat in a chair – it was covered in soot. All the upstairs of our house was damaged. I remember later being schooled in peoples' houses with a few more children and a teacher. As children we enjoyed playing 'house' in the air raid shelter."

Saturday, 14th Dec

STILL LIFE! Still life all right but no club, no city, no café "no nothings" Home for tea. First time home since about war started.

Mike Lawton:

"At the time of the Blitz my mum, Rose Lawton, was 15 and lived with her parents, Grace and Andrew Reynolds, on Everingham Road, Southey Green, along with her sister Mary, plus brothers Andrew and John. There had been previous air raid alerts but it was thought the German planes had been on reconnaissance missions. When the raid came it was in the middle of winter and was pitch black, made even darker by the fact all of the lights were out. Not long after the sirens made their mournful wail, the sound of the first wave of bombers reached our ears. Rose's mother had them all crammed under the kitchen table in the dark – how much good that would have done them in the event of a bomb dropping - doesn't bear thinking about. It seemed an eternally long night with the raid finishing just after 4am.

"They didn't know where the bombs had dropped so dressed for work after a sleepless night. Rose was employed as a cutlery worker at Needham, Veall & Tyzack on Milton Street and was due to start work at 8am. At the bus stop on Moonshine Lane she met up with two friends. No bus came so they thought they'd better walk. Their walk took them over Shirecliffe, along Burngreave Road and down Spital Hill towards the Wicker. The Wicker Arches had large wooden doors on them and they were closed. The girls had no idea what lay beyond them. They passed through the door on the pavement and could scarely believe their eyes at the scenes of utter devastation. The most incredible sight was that of an Intake tram that had been sliced in two. The bodies of two people that had been travelling on it were still there. No resources had been available to remove them at that point.

"One of the policemen on duty with the firemen came over to ask where they were going. His face was black from clouds of dust. Rose distinctly remembered the white lines that steaked his face – either from sweat, tears or both. He said they needed to be careful as they walked as many more bombs had been dropped in the direction they were going. Buildings were unsafe and there was falling debris. Rose left her friends near the markets area and saw the damaged buildings as she looked up King Street. The Marples Hotel had been completely flattened. The journey up High Street, along Fargate and down The Moor brought further scenes of devastation. She began to wonder if her place of work was still there. She breathed a sigh of relief when she saw it was.

"She doesn't recall how much work was done that day but, after it, she had another very long walk home."

Connie Bentley:

"I remember going up to school and there being this dead man and a child laid on this bench; first time I'd seen anything like that."

Doris Butler (From Walkley project):

"We had a canary at that time and this canary sung through all that noise of banging and guns."

John Unsworth:

"Many who were 'bombed out' of their homes and were unable to stay with relatives or friends, were taken to reception centres, usually schools, where they were given blankets and food. In at least one reception centre, food was cooked on a field kitchen."

Mr E Walker:

"I remember going to town and seeing bodies outside Marples and damage down the Moor. My brother was in Marples and came out thirty minutes before it dropped. All his pals were killed."

Jo Borthen:

"My Mum, now 95 years old, walked from home on Montgomery Road, Netheredge, to the insurance office she worked in behind the cathedral. The office had been bombed so the workers took the intact paperwork back to the boss' home in Abbey Lane I believe. After the war, she went back to work there as all the jobs were kept open."

December 13th	Ecclesall Junior School - - Last night Sheffield suffered from a terrible air raid. On reaching school this a.m. we had 41 children present, so I closed school until Monday. Mrs Walker's house - one of the staff - was damaged during raid.

CHAPTER 7

Sheffield Blitz - Day two
December 15th, 1940

Sunday, 15th Dec

Out visiting. Fire near them, sirens at 1pm. Heard a plane, which dropped two bombs at Oughtibridge before sirens. All clear about 1.30pm. 7pm sirens came again and gunfire. Nearly as bad for us, but worse in the East of Sheffield. They have come back to finish off the works. Not quite managed it tho!

The second night of the Sheffield Blitz was far less intense than the first. It lasted 3 hours and 35 minutes. It was far more concentrated on the industrial East End – site of Sheffield's armaments production.

Mrs E:

"When the bombers came over the second time they came near Ravencarr Road where my sister-in-law lived and a bullet went right through her big bedroom window and through a jug and bowl."

Pat Furniss:

"Remember mum telling us (they lived in Attercliffe) that nan had baked some breadcakes and left them at the cellar head to cool as they went into the cellar when the siren went off. Mum decided to venture up the stairs to butter those breadcakes, and as she was doing them there was a whistle of a large bomb coming closer. She jumped from top to bottom of cellar steps and still had butter on her knife. It's just a lighter note on what was harrowing times.

"A lot of my relatives worked at Brown Baileys during the war and my mum worked on an overhead crane (although she later was afraid of heights). I remember my little nannan telling me when she went for a job there to meet the criteria you had to be able to lift a shell with both hands."

Monday, 16th Dec	Just entering my diary when ?-? sirens, but all clear. Never heard the alarm. 9.05pm to 9.45pm. Worked today, and finished at 4pm.
Tuesday, 17th Dec	"He hath prepared a city for them" - a city? Not a home or a place. They will sure need a city. Went to Endcliffe (Thomas Ward lived at Endcliffe and Mildred used to go to the house when required to do personal work for the family.) Plane over this afternoon. Sirens at 2pm. Did not go to work this afternoon. They were all in shelters. All clear at 4.15pm. None at night.
Wednesday, 18th Dec	Finished work at 4.30pm until Jan 31st. Planes over late last night, nothing heard. No sirens.
Friday, 20th Dec	Sirens 7pm to 1.00am. No bombs, gunfire round Kiveton Park Way.
Saturday, 21st Dec	Sirens 6.30pm to 4.05am. Planes and gunfire, no bombs. Black-out 5.18am. Royal Bus Co (?) still smoking furiously.
Sunday, 22nd Dec	Up late, bed all day with cold. Sirens 6.30pm to 10.30pm, guns, no bombs. Again at 1am to 6.30am
Monday, 23rd Dec	Black-out at 5.19pm, 7.10pm to 1.30am planes, but no bombs.
Wednesday 25th Dec	MILDRED'S BIRTHDAY. She enters in her diary "Peaceful night"
Wednesday, 1st Jan	Crossley's shop in town still smoking since 13th. Sirens 6.30pm to 7.00pm again, 10.30pm to 2.10am. Many passing over, but no bombs.

Sirens then followed on the following nights, but no bombs: 3rd Jan, 4th Jan, 5th Jan, 9th Jan.

Devonshire Green

One of the biggest combined losses of life occurred in the Devonshire Green area of the city centre. This was a thriving community of back-to-back housing. This was virtually razed to the ground in the Blitz. Today it is landscaped park known simply as Devonshire Green.

Tragic death of family that fled to Sheffield for safety

"My grandparents never spoke of the time when their daughters died in the war. I cannot remember how old I was when I first heard about the death of my father's younger sisters and saw a photograph of two little girls who would have been my aunts if they had lived. Over the years I have heard more details of events in Sheffield on the night of December 12th,1940 and told the story to my children. My son Matthew and I visited Sheffield with my father, Leon, in 2006 and went to the city cemetery to see the communal grave for those killed by enemy action, and to Devonshire Green where Lily (Family Photo 1), Eileen and Doris (Family Photo 2) were killed in the Sheffield Blitz.

"My father's story began in May 1940 when a telegram was delivered to his home in Gosport, across the harbour from the naval dockyard at Portsmouth. He was aged 13 at the time and ran to his Aunt Rose's house to find his mother. She was at the local British Legion with his sisters and he gave them the telegram. His father was serving on a destroyer, HMS Wessex, in the English Channel and they feared bad news. The telegram had been sent by his father; he was safe and in Portsmouth and he wanted them to bring him some clothes so that he could come home. His ship had been bombarding enemy troops and equipment near Calais and came under attack by dive bombers and was hit by three bombs and sunk. Survivors were picked up by another destroyer and brought back to England. Leon's father, Eugene, had experienced first-hand the destructive power of bombing and with the fear of invasion on the south coast during the summer of 1940, Leon and his sisters, Doris aged 12 and Eileen aged 10, were sent north to Sheffield to stay with Eugene's cousin and his wife, Fred and Pat Ashton, in Fulwood. Leon remembers attending Greystones School and his sisters went to Nether Green School. His father was posted to HMS Queen Elizabeth, a battleship, at Portsmouth which was later sent to Rosyth in Scotland during December 1940 and his mother was serving in the Wrens in Gosport.

"During December, Fred's wife Pat was admitted to hospital for a short time. Doris and Eileen went to stay with their grandmother, Lily Leclere, at 174 Devonshire Street where she lived above her baker's shop. Leon was sent to live with Fred's mother and father, Sarah and Jim Ashton, in Burngreave Road, Pitsmoor. Uncle Jim was a buyer at Cockaynes in the city and Leon remembers he was a very keen Sheffield United supporter and could always be found at Bramall Lane for home matches. Leon was

Family Photo 1:
Lilly Leclere (née Shaw).

with Aunty Sarah and Uncle Jim on the evening of December 12th, 1940 and remembers the sound of bombs falling and exploding in the city. Pat Ashton was due to come home from hospital on December 13th and Leon was expecting to go back to Fred and Pat's home with his sisters.

"The next day, Leon was aware that something had happened and remembers being taken in Fred Ashton's car to a street near his grandmother's house and left there for a while. He found out that 174 Devonshire Street had been hit by a bomb during the night and the building was a complete wreck and his grandmother and two sisters were missing. My father believes Published Photo 1 shows the wreckage of the building where Lily was living and his sisters, Doris and Eileen, were staying at the time of the Sheffield Blitz and is sure that 174 Devonshire Street is just below the bottom of the picture, below the label for Eldon St in Published Photo 2. He was taken to the wrecked house and asked if he could find the entrance to the coal hole in the back yard which led to the cellar that was used as a shelter. He could not find it. Leon remembers there was an unexploded bomb nearby and it was not safe to stay near the house and search for his sisters and grandmother. The last time Leon saw his grandmother and sisters alive was a few days before the Sheffield Blitz when they all went to the cinema to see 'The Wizard of Oz.'

"Leon's father was granted compassionate leave from his ship and arrived in Sheffield soon after the attacks. Leon remembers the day his father arrived in Sheffield as the saddest day in his life. Leon thinks it was his father who located the entrance to the cellar and found the bodies of his mother (Lily's death certificate states her body was found on 18 December 1940) and his two daughters. The body of Frederick Mallam, aged 80, who was a lodger at 174 Devonshire Street was also found in the cellar. Leon's mother arrived in Sheffield a couple of days later and he recalls there had been a difficulty contacting her in Gosport. Leon does not remember attending a burial or funeral at the communal grave at the city cemetery. His father remained in Sheffield for a week before re-joining his ship. Leon and his mother, also called Lily, remained in Sheffield for 18 months and then returned to Gosport.

"Eugene returned to HMS Queen Elizabeth at Rosyth and, after the completion of the ships modernisation and sea trials, returned to active duty and by May 1941 had joined the Mediterranean Fleet at Alexandria. In December 1941 Italian divers placed explosive charges beneath HMS Queen Elizabeth and other ships in Alexandria harbour. The charge

Family Photo 2:
Eileen (left) and Doris Leclere.

exploded below the boiler room causing serious damage and Eugene suffered internal injuries swallowing fuel oil as he was leaving the damaged boiler room. Following emergency treatment for his stomach he recovered from his injuries. After initial repairs HMS Queen Elizabeth sailed to South Africa and later crossed the Atlantic to Norfolk, Virginia for repairs and refit. Eugene eventually returned to England with an Atlantic convoy and after the end of the war he left the Royal Navy and worked at Priddy's Hard (naval munitions yard) at Gosport. Leon and his mother stayed in Gosport and survived the regular air raids over Portsmouth and Gosport. Leon joined the Royal Navy for national

Family Photo 3:
Eugene, Lily and Leon Leclere in 1947.

Service in 1945 and served in the Fleet Air Arm in the Far East until the surrender of Japan. He returned home to his parents in Gosport in 1947 (Family Photo 3)."

Sheila Cutts:

"It smelled like Bonfire Night and everything was in chaos. You could smell the bombs and the fire. The Germans had dropped incendiary bombs just above the Cathedral. It was chaos you didn't know where you were walking - nowhere looked the same."

John Unsworth:

"During the blitz and other air raids, we settled down in the cellar on wooden bunks reading and playing board games while my father went to his Air Raid Precaution post in Tullibardine Road. The wardens patrolled the area looking for incendiary bombs with buckets of sand, shovels and stirrup pumps ready in strategic places, and were ready to aid people who may have been trapped or were in difficulty. After the blitz, I went out collecting shrapnel from the bombs. We were very lucky in that we did not receive any damage. All our windows had been overlaid with a heavy mesh to prevent injury should they be blown in, making us live in a perpetual twilight.

Jean M. Tomlinson:

"I was a little girl living in Staniforth Road, Darnall, and my father was a policeman at Attercliffe Police Station. Whenever the sirens went, policemen were immediately on duty and he would go, leaving my mother to see my brother and I into the shelter – not knowing when (or if) we would see him again."

Brave scouts were key part of the relief efforts

With only a saucepan for protection against the might of German Luftwaffe – this photo became one of the most striking images from the Sheffield Blitz in December 1940.

So much so that Boy Scout John Flinn — who only had the cooking utensil to protect his head from flying shrapnel and collapsing buildings — was awarded a medal for his gallantry and is now a major part of the city's new exhibition to the attacks.

John Flinn and his scouting colleague John Cotton, were both awarded the Gilt Cross for their bravery – a medal which is still given today.

John Flinn was a member of the 36th Sheffield (St Johns Ranmoor) group and received his coveted award in April 1941 "for his gallantry and resource in rendering valuable assistance at firefighting and resource work during a heavy air raid on Sheffield."

He worked all night to douse incendiary bombs, deal with a fractured gas main, and rescue an injured woman from falling bomb shrapnel. He commandeered a grocer's barrow and pushed her to the warden post.

When John dashed home, during a lull in the bombing to reassure his parents he was okay, he arrived just in time to put out a fire. He then returned to his post.

Hundreds of scouts were on duty right across the city in World War Two.

Hero boy scout
John Flinn.

CHAPTER 8

The clean up
December 16th, 1940

The Aftermath

Over 2,000 dead and wounded. 300,000 people without water. 200 craters in the city's roads. 106 schools damaged. 30,000 homes damaged – 1,000 flattened. 31 trams damaged.

Over 23,000 people taken to rest centres. 12,732 billeted. 4,000 evacuated to other towns.

90 fire engines and 680 men from 28 different towns and city's all came to Sheffield's aid over those two nights.

A tram is ripped in two.

Betty McMahon (courtesy of the Walkley Historians):

"In between times after the big air raid, my aunties were all bombed, they lived at Darnall, their houses weren't demolished but the roofs were blown off and so I can visualise them now, coming up the road with a little suitcase and just the clothes that they'd got on, sort of thing. And we put everybody up here for one night and then a couple of my aunties went to relatives but my auntie and uncle with the two children stayed here. They were here over Christmas, probably for about a couple of months till they got their roofs back on again.

That was quite sad, y'know the fact that their house had been bombed and I thought that's an awful thing to happen."

Jim Simmons:

"I said 'Why have they bombed Sheffield? I thought they were bombing t' steel factories?' And dad says, 'Well, somebody's miscalculated it', which they must have done because if they'd have done that damage to Sheffield, in t' factories, then there'd be no factories left!"

Damage to Northend Printers, West Street.

Redgates toyshop in flames along with the rest of Moorhead.

Top: The King and Queen visit the bombed out city

Right: The King and Queen chat to survivors.

Below: Damage to the Devonshire Green area.

CHAPTER 9

Christmas dinner
for the homeless

It's hard to imagine what kind of festive cheer the people of Sheffield managed to conjure up for December 25th, 1940.

Great swathes of the city lay in ruins, there were few people that hadn't be affected by the death of loved ones, friends or work colleagues and tens of thousands were homeless and living in temporary accommodation.

Over 300,000 people were without water, 50 electricity sub stations were out of action and more than 3,000 telephone lines were damaged.

Much of the city centre lay in ruins along with homegrown department stores like Redgates, Walsh's, Cockaynes and Atkinsons. A total of 1,200 shops and business premises were totally destroyed.

Wartime censorship forbade full details of casualties and damage being published immediately. This led to widespread rumours of a death toll far higher than the actual one, later stated as over 660 with hundreds more injured.

The threat of a full scale German invasion was still a very real one.

Christmas was actually one of the few traditions that survived in the war in some shape or form. Guy Fawkes' Night was banned immediately, as gunpowder production was needed for the war effort and bonfires contravened the blackout.

Hundreds spent Christmas sleeping at High Storrs School which became a rest shelter.

One chink of the spirit of Christmas came in the shape of Sheffield City Hall. They provided Christmas dinner for the homeless. They opened a restaurant providing reasonably priced food for the rest of the war.

A scene from Shiregreen.

Some parents, unsure if their family would survive the intense bombing, decided to bring Christmas forward.

Jean Tomlinson: "Christmas was really strange. We had some friends who lived just up the road. I think they were some distant relatives of ours. The children received their Christmas presents immediately after the first night of the Blitz. They said, 'We may not be here at Christmas so have your presents now.'

But her father was having none of it.

"'No, no, Christmas is Christmas' he said. We had Christmas at Christmas but other people didn't."

Emergency services struggled to cope

Elaborate planning had been arranged to accommodate 10,000 bombed out Sheffielders if the worst happened and the city was badly hit. Another 1,600 volunteers had been enrolled and trained up and attached to rest centres and feeding stations.

But as the January 1941 edition of 'All Clear', the ARP newsletter, said, the service could not cope. "...no scheme could have anticipated the ghastly setbacks which this service suffered. The headquarters of the organising body obtained three direct hits. Over 75 per cent of the centres had been rendered untenable. At one time over 23,000 persons were present in the temporary centres.

"Many members of the staff and of the voluntary personnel were themselves homeless- but they carried on."

What the service achieved was incredible considering the circumstances. Over 60,000 hot meals were distributed within 24 hours of the 'all clear' from one institution alone.

Within hours, a host of alternative rest premises were secured including schoolrooms, church halls, clubs, picture houses and more.

Medical services were badly hit. Four of the largest hospitals in the city

Hillsborough Tabernackle that was hit in the Blitz.

were damaged in the raids and large quantities of medical supplies destroyed.

Mobile canteens appeared from Manchester, Leeds, Wakefield and Bradford to help feed the hungry alongside vehicles from the Church Army, the Salvation Army and others.

Hundreds of homes across the city opened their doors to the homeless.

'All Clear' said: "The spirit of Sheffield was clearly displayed by the numerous offers made to provide accommodation."

Memorial service held on the site of the Coleford Road Warden's Post in December 1941 – a year after the loss of ten lives on the site.

Robert Wilkinson:

"Mother was a wonderful cook, and despite rationing she produced some lovely meals, yes it seemed pretty normal. Of course there were power cuts and that sort of thing and hurricane lamps, you know the power went off the power came back on again, but I cant remember it being particularly miserable or anything like that."

Clockwise from bottom left:
Bomb damage on The Moor; Damage to Bramall Lane; A Christmas message from Atkinsons department store which was flattened in the attacks.

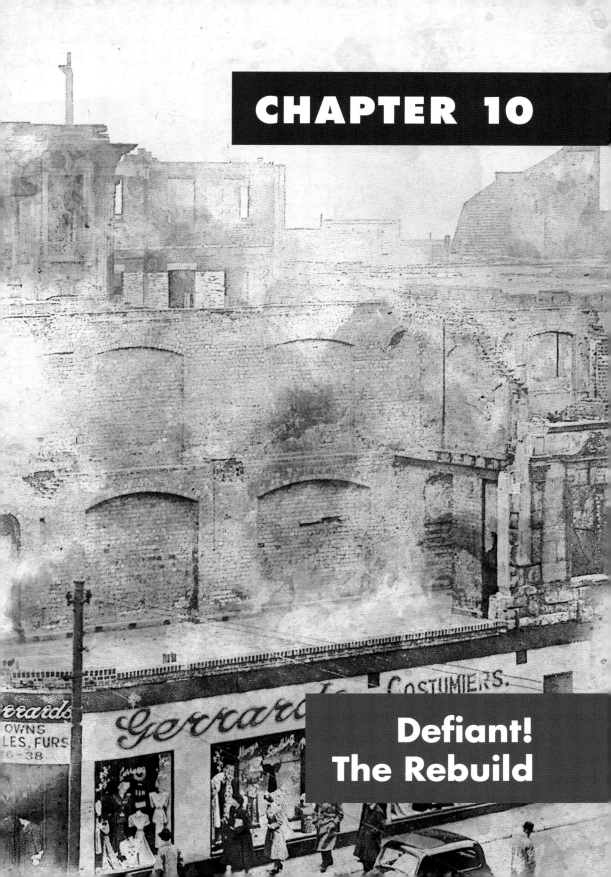

CHAPTER 10

Defiant!
The Rebuild

The rebuild was a massive operation. Builders, joiners and craftspeople were enlisted from right across the region as they worked on the stricken city.

Bombsites became a familiar site. Some lasted years, even decades.

Atkinsons department store, which was razed to the ground on the first night of the Sheffield Blitz, didn't unveil its new store until 1960 – a full twenty years after the bombing. And theirs wasn't an isolated story.

All Clear – the ARP newsletter produced throughout the war in the city.

1940 (January 8th)	Clifford Church of England School, Psalter Lane - School closed a.m. - after heavy air raid on Sheffield previous night 11 children present sent home. Damage done to the school by shrapnel 1-hall roof riddled with holes. Seven windows broken & ten cracked.
1941,21 January	Ecclesall Junior School - We opened school this a.m. after 5 weeks closure, owing to the Blitz. Teachers were employed in "rest centres" etc caring for the homeless.

Damage on High Street.

Top: Walsh's department store on High Street before the Blitz.
Bottom: The shell of Walsh's after it was bombed.

CHAPTER 11

December 24th, 1944 – First (and last) flying bomb lands over Sheffield

Above: Bomb damage to Hawksley Avenue in the Hillsborough area of Sheffield.
Opposite, top to bottom: Gathering possessions from their bombed out houses;
Damage to the Devonshire Green area; Bramall Lane was hit in the attacks.

The air raid alert rang out from 5.15am until 6.20am. It signalled the arrival of the first (and last) flying bomb over Sheffield. It landed in a field in the Beighton area.

Sheffield had 136 air raid alerts in total in World War Two – around a dozen of those were in daylight hours.

The final one lasted 46 minutes and was on March 4th, 1945.

Every single month of 1941, barring December, had air raid warnings.

Bomb damage to
Deacon's Bank, The Moor.

CHAPTER 12

December 24th,
VE Day

VE Day (Victory In Europe Day) came on May 8th, 1945. Britain had been at war for nearly six years. This was the day the Allies accepted the unconditional surrender of the armed forces of Nazi Germany and the Third Reich. Adolf Hitler had shot himself just days earlier in his Berlin bunker.

VE Day celebrations on Fargate.

The sacrifices of Sheffield and the country had not been in vain.

The Blitz might have destroyed much of the physical heart of the city but it didn't break its spirit. If anything it made it more resilient.

The steelworks went on working throughout the war, much of them operated by the women of the city whilst the men fought at the frontline.

Nearly 80 years since the Sheffield Blitz, and it's hard to imagine the horrors and sacrifices endured by the people of the city on those two nights in December 1940, and throughout the whole six years of war.

It was their spirit – and the spirit of counterparts in other bombed cities like Birmingham, Liverpool, Bristol, Southampton, Plymouth, Coventry and London – that helped carry the country to victory.

The war in the Far East continued until August 14th, 1945, when the Japanese surrendered and WW2, the most devastating conflict in the history of mankind, was finally over.

The bombed out Arnold Laver building.

CHAPTER 13

February 2017 – The unveiling of the city's first permanent exhibition to the Sheffield Blitz

If you want to find out more about the attacks you should visit the exhibition that came about as a direct result of this project.

It is housed in Sheffield's National Emergency Services Museum on Shalesmoor.

The last surviving fire engine that fought the Blitz fires in December 1940 is amongst the scores of artefacts that make up the collection.

The historic Leyland was rushed into the city from nearby Barnsley and stayed in service in Sheffield until the late 1950s.

The exhibition contains scores of rare and original Blitz-related objects and photos, Second World War emergency vehicles, oral history recordings from survivors, film footage as well as the fire brigade's original map of bomb sites across the city.

The exhibition was created by Bill Bevan of *in*Heritage with the museum.

Below: The only surviving engine that fought the Sheffield Blitz fires that takes pride of place in the permanent exhibition.

Opposite, top left: The media turned out in force to cover the opening of the exhibition.

Opposite, top right and bottom: The Sheffield Blitz exhibition.

Museum visitor numbers have doubled since it was unveiled.

The Sheffield Blitz exhibition is open during the normal opening hours of the National Emergency Services Museum. There is an admission charge.

More information on the National Emergency Services Museum from: www.emergencymuseum.org.uk

You should also visit the Sheffield Blitz exhibition that is housed at South Yorkshire Aircraft Museum in Doncaster.

More information from: https://www.southyorkshireaircraftmuseum.org.uk

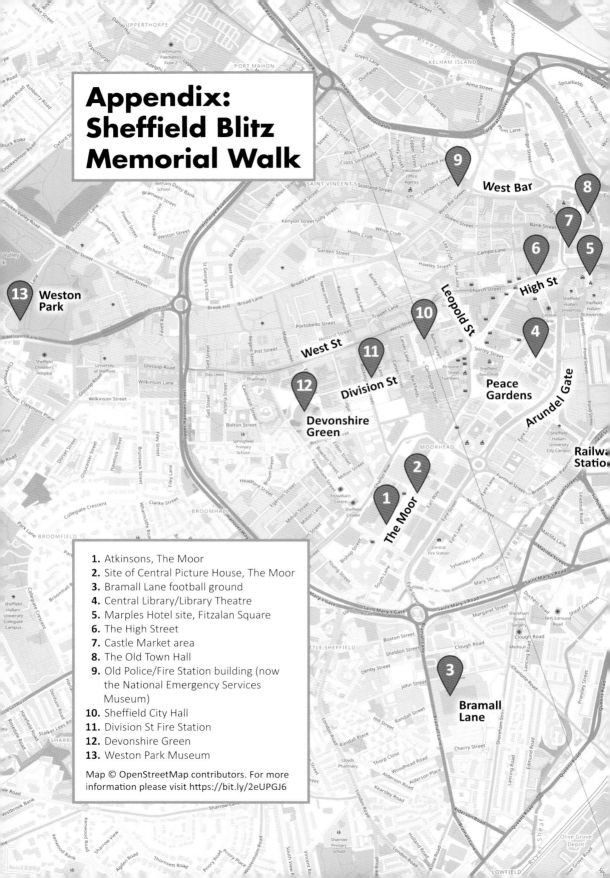

Appendix: Sheffield Blitz Memorial Walk

1. Atkinsons, The Moor
2. Site of Central Picture House, The Moor
3. Bramall Lane football ground
4. Central Library/Library Theatre
5. Marples Hotel site, Fitzalan Square
6. The High Street
7. Castle Market area
8. The Old Town Hall
9. Old Police/Fire Station building (now the National Emergency Services Museum)
10. Sheffield City Hall
11. Division St Fire Station
12. Devonshire Green
13. Weston Park Museum

Map © OpenStreetMap contributors. For more information please visit https://bit.ly/2eUPGJ6

1) Atkinsons, The Moor.

The only independent department store left in Sheffield that survived the Blitz. The Moor was one of the most devastated areas of the city on the 12th and required many of the city's fire fighters. Atkinson's original building was flattened – the present one was opened in 1960.

2) Site of Central Picture House, The Moor.

Scores of families were packed in here watching Shirley Temple in Bluebird. Kids remember sheltering under billiard table downstairs, eventually had to leave during blitz and witness what many describe as 'the holocaust on the Moor' with much of the area a blazing inferno.

3) Bramall Lane football ground.

The ground and stand suffered significant damage, with bomb craters across the pitch. There is an iconic photograph of one of the goalposts in ruins. Bombs dropped across the entire area around the ground.

4) Central Library/Library Theatre.

This was the hub of the relief effort. Thousands of people gathered here for information about rehoming, food, lost relatives, lost power and more.

5) Marples Hotel site, Fitzalan Square.

The Marples received a direct hit at 11:44pm killing the majority of the people inside. Scene of the single biggest loss of life. Bodies are stil buried underneath.

6) The High Street.

There was a direct hit to C&A Modes and Walsh's department stores. The High Street was another area where Sheffield's fire fighters concentrated their work. A famous photograph shows burnt out trams on the street. This image became synonymous with the Sheffield Blitz.

7) Castle Market area.

The old market was devastated. After the war, the market was rebuilt as a vast concrete building, which has since been demolished with the market's relocation to the Moor.

8) The Old Town Hall.

The basement of the town hall was a wartime telephone communications centre with a massive switchboard. The centre was full of staff on the night of the 12th December and had a direct hit, setting fire to the roof. Sheffield fire fighter Doug Lightning led the response on extinguished the fire, receiving a round of applause from the staff.

9) Old Police/Fire Station building (now National Emergency Services Museum).

Another hub of activity on both nights of the Sheffield Blitz. You can visit the Sheffield Blitz Gallery here, see fire fighting equipment from the city and enter an emergency vehicle and an Anderson Shelter. You can also here eye-witness accounts of the Blitz from Sheffield residents and Doug Lightning, a Blitz fire fighter. Entry fee charged.

10) Sheffield City Hall.

One of the few places you can still see shrapnel damage. An emergency water tank in Barker's Pool shielded much of the blast as a ballroom dance continued downstairs.

11) Division St Fire Station.

This fire station, now a bar, was central to the fire fighting response to the Blitz. Crews of the city's professional fire service spread out across Sheffield from here. They fought the flames

---

Defiance in the face of Southey Hill parachute mine damage.

against unimaginable odds and amongst dropping bombs and explosions for over 12 hours without break, drink or food.

12) Devonshire Green.

A whole community of back-to-back housing was wiped out just off Division Street. Rather than rebuilding homes, the city council kept the area as an open park and so Devonshire Green was created. A make- shift mortuary was erected with bodies from Marples Hotel brought here.

13) Weston Park Museum.

Half of ornate Victorian Mappin Art Gallery was destroyed by a bomb landing in Mushroom Lane. Much of the museum was also damaged, including a collection of Blue John which had just been put out on display. A fireball went down one of the corridors, damaging some of their exhibits.

Contributions/thanks

To the following Sheffield Blitz 75th volunteers who helped put this book together via research, attending meetings and interviewing survivors:
Sarah Armstrong, Don Ash, Hilary Bull, Julie Clark, Chris Kolonko, Alan Turner, Leigh Turner, Ian Wilshaw.

To the following who had belief in our project and helped get it off the ground:
Nicholas Atkinson, Sandra Barley, Terry Deary, and Graham Frith, Peter Stringfellow.

To the Sheffield Blitz 75th team: Neil Anderson, Bill Bevan and Richard Godley.

To the following that have all provided help and support throughout this project:
Julia Armstrong and all at The Star, Cheryl Bailey, Jenny Bland, Frank Donnelly, Nik Farah, John Garrett and all at SUFC, Frank Reininghaus, Martin Geller, Phil Jarvis and all at South Yorkshire Aircraft Museum, Beth Keever, Lorna Kirwan, Tim Knebel and all at Sheffield Archives and Local Studies, Mike Lawton, Mike Leclere, Doug Lightning (RIP), Julie Lightning Shaw, Dave McCarthy, Michelle McDonald, Dave Manvell, Clara Morgan, Martin Ross, Angela Treweek, Matt Wakefield and everyone at the National Emergency Services Museum, Julie Wilson, Frank Yates.

To the names that will live on through this project: Mabel Dean, George Herbert Lawrence, Rose Lawton, Doris Leclere, Lily Leclere, Eileen Leclere, Douglas Lightning, Alfred Theodore Bentley.

Sheffield Blitz roll of honour

Kevin Briggs	Freda Jarvis	Kath Peters
Steve Bush	Lorna Kirwan	Angela Treweek
Janet Clark	Mike Lawton	Helen West-Ward
Paul Clark	Brian Norie	Barbara Wilkes
Beryl Garner	Brenda Percival	
Horace Gill	George Percival	

The Sheffield Blitz Group